EXPERIENCE THINKING

Creating Connected Experiences

TEDDE VAN GELDEREN

Experience Thinking

Creating Connected Experiences

ISBN 978161961616271

Design by Akendi

Creative Direction Athena Herrmann
Art Direction Siobhan Kennedy
Design Amanda Billark

Akendi

Thank you!

I'd like to thank Anneke for her support and her help in keeping things in perspective. Thanks also go to the editorial team—Kathleen, Emily, Dave, and Brad—for their enthusiasm in guiding me through the publishing process. And I'd like to thank all Akendians, present and past, plus my old colleagues throughout my career who helped shape the thinking that is captured here. Through conversations, in meetings, during presentations, and at Friday lunches, each nudged this book further. Many thanks!

TABLE OF CONTENTS

Introduction   1

The Experience Matters   3

This Book is for You   5

Part One – Experience Thinking: The Concept

Chapter 1: Start with the Experience   11

Chapter 2: Think You Don't Need an Experience Strategy?   31

Part Two – About Experience Thinking

Chapter 3: Structure: People, Business, Process, & Technology   43

Chapter 4: The Experience Thinking Framework   51

Chapter 5: Experience Thinking for Brand   57

Chapter 6: The Engagement Experience   77

Chapter 7: Experience Thinking for Product   83

Chapter 8: Experience Thinking for Content   101

Chapter 9: Experience Thinking for Service   121

Part Three – Experience Lifecycle Planning

Chapter 10: Designing for the End-to-End Experience Lifecycle   145

Part Four – Implementation: Applying Experience Thinking

Chapter 11: Engagement Strategies for Experience Thinking   167

Chapter 12: Embracing Experience Thinking   175

INTRODUCTION

"Hi, my name is Matt."

The words baffled me. I was at the airport, renting a car, as I've done a hundred times. Faced with a barrage of rental companies promising similar services, I'd walked up to one counter, expecting the usual treatment.

You know how it goes. You walk up to a counter and start answering questions for the attendant's forms. You show your license and sign on the dotted line.

This time, however, the rental agent stuck out his hand and introduced himself. There was none of the usual hurry or annoyance—just a simple, friendly greeting before any attempt was made to establish a business connection.

Matt's moment of connection seemed out of place in the middle of the basic transaction of my car rental. What should have been a dry and impersonal process immediately changed when he said his name, connected physically by shaking my hand, and paid attention to me as a person. I was invited into a relationship of sorts from the very beginning of the transaction.

Personal interaction wasn't an afterthought; it was implemented by design. The company had done its homework, and it had taken the time to determine my wants and needs as a prospective client. Matt's small act completely changed my perception and my *experience* of renting a car with that particular company.

THE EXPERIENCE MATTERS

Experiences are vital, and they are the answer to questions such as these: How do I engage my audience? Will my customer ever become a user? How can I move my user into the category of loyal client?

I answer product and service design questions every day and help organizations deliver better business results through better experiences. Using an approach that I call "Experience Thinking," organizations can direct their efforts in strategy, research, and design to lead to long-term customer relationships—and more revenue.

The good news is that you don't have to work with a consultant like me to realize the benefits of Experience Thinking, or the principles that are part of this "experience design." My goal in writing this book is to help and empower you with a more holistic perspective on creating experiences. I offer a design process that you can manage on your own in the end.

Developing a product or service from the experiential perspective isn't just a good idea or an opportunity to make audiences feel good— it has become essential. Experiences need to deliver from start to finish. Paying attention to the experience has become increasingly necessary because today's users *expect* a cohesive experience journey. If they don't get it from you, they'll move on until they find it.

THIS BOOK IS FOR YOU

This is a book for people who create and build things and who want to create remarkable experiences for their audience. Whether you're creating digital products, physical products, or services, Experience Thinking introduces a balanced left- and right-brain approach to your experience creation process.

Experience Thinking applies in many design situations. It helps code, hardware, and content developers move from creating what is feasible to creating what delivers impact.

Designers of sites have to be aware of their audience expectations and experience using the sites they develop. The magnitude of content, particularly on government websites, inherently makes the process of discovering information more difficult.

If you work in the tech field in one way or another, Experience Thinking allows you to create the experience on paper first, and then test it with customers and users, before jumping headfirst into the functionality building. By working through the design in this way, from the position of the user's experience, you expose potential

Experience Thinking starts by delaying the technology-building piece and focusing first on the experience.

problems early, before they create major issues once the product is launched.

In the B2B (business-to-business) world, if you focus on the experience, you can first determine if an idea, product, or service is ultimately viable. For example, a company adding a new technology product to their line might start with functional requirements. In contrast, after interviews and validation exercises, you might (or might not) prove the product *before* you invest in it and design it. Creating the experience first is instrumental for early stage validation and helps you avoid building something that ultimately no one wants.

People who build things that have a spatial element will also benefit from paying early attention to the experience. For example, how do visitors know where to go in a hospital? Is the experience different for patients than it is for visitors? What happens when you walk into a space that is highly emotional? These are only a few of the aspects you'd need to consider, in addition to base functionality and use.

Anyone who designs and builds products and services will benefit from the Experience Thinking approach. Put the experience first, not the software or the technology or even the business. Start with the intended experience, and take the impact of the experience on other factors seriously. Let the experience be the driving force behind your strategic decisions.

The experience matters. It's good for your audience, and it's good for your business. Once you understand and embrace the concepts of Experience Thinking, you will be able to transform your product-focused organization into one that is audience-focused and primed for repeatable success.

So why wouldn't you do this?

PART ONE

Experience Thinking: The Concept

Chapter 1

START WITH THE EXPERIENCE

Experience is a big word. My experience of renting a car was much more than filling out a form and walking away with the keys. It involved my total immersion in the moment. I wasn't just renting a car at an airport; I was experiencing the composite of everything around me.

You encounter experiences on a daily basis. It could be your commute to work or a wait at the subway station. Experiences happen in a space or environment. While in the environment, you may be using a product. The product might be a newspaper, or a cell phone, or even a space such as a café or coffee shop. These things are all part of your experience. For each of these touch points, or more accurately experience points, your experience with that particular thing is made up of a set of events as you go through time.

The experience is a holistic view of how we interact with our surroundings.

In the world of design, experience can be understood in the same way: its a holistic view of how we interact with our surroundings. Both tangible and intangible characteristics make up an experience, because every experience point is funneled through our senses.

An experience may be triggered by the senses and then funneled through such cognitive processes as awareness, thought, and observation, but there are a multitude of other levels at work. To *design* for these experiences, we need to take many aspects into account.

Experience Characteristics

In order to design using this holistic approach, you need to design for all of the characteristics and experience components from the start of the experience to the end. The elements of experience are all connected—or they should be. For example, an organization may want to "fix" its software, but the software exists on a device and may be connected to in-person customer service provided by the organization. If you simply work on the software, the focus is on only one element of the problem. Neglecting the other elements creates a breakdown in the experience. This brokenness can overshadow the whole experience.

EMOTION

The feelings generated by experiences in a given situation.

INTENSITY

A flash moment or total immersion in the experience.

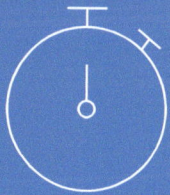

TIMING

The amount of time, from seconds to decades, in which the events in the experience occur.

COVERAGE

The number of products or services that are needed in the experience and its environment.

INTERACTION

The participatory aspect of experience gained through an interaction with a product, service, or person.

MEANING

The experience can be symbolic, pragmatic, or semantic.

Experience Components

Another way to understand experiences in the context of holistic design is to look at the three major components of every experience.

PEOPLE

The "people" component is made up of customers, users, and clients, depending on where they are on the timeline of the experience.

Stop thinking about just the 'customer'.

ACTIVITIES

The "activity" component is all of the things you do with a product, content, service, or a combination thereof that are part of the experience.

PLACES

The "place" component is a combination of all of the components that together form one event, in one location, in one defined, physical environment.

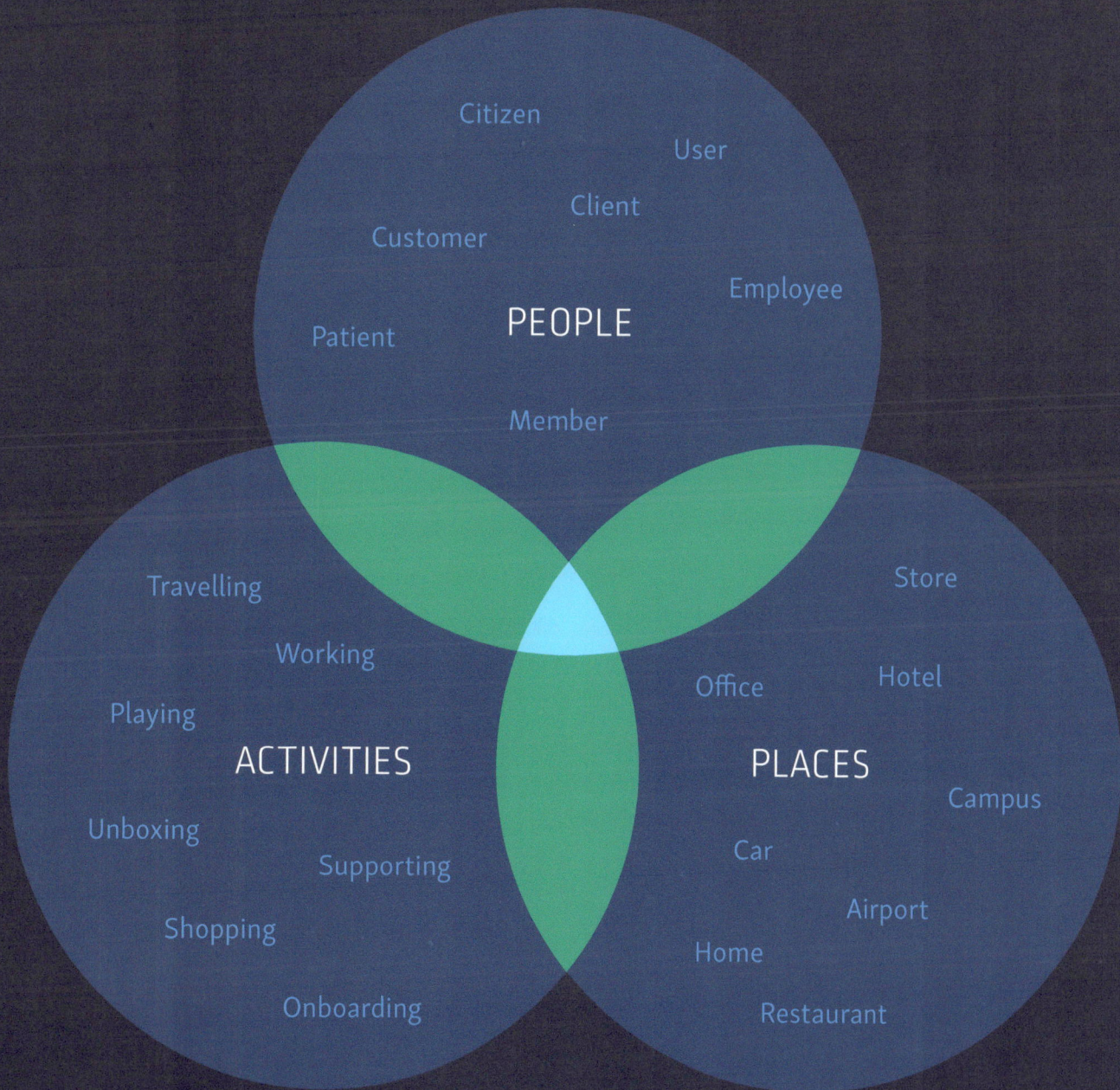

PEOPLE

Citizen
User
Client
Customer
Employee
Patient
Member

ACTIVITIES

Travelling
Working
Playing
Unboxing
Supporting
Shopping
Onboarding

PLACES

Store
Office
Hotel
Campus
Car
Airport
Home
Restaurant

DESIGN HOLISTICALLY

Experience Thinking

The concept of experience design takes all of the components of an experience into consideration. Experience Thinking gives you a framework for planning experience design in your organization. It fosters a mindset, or a way of looking at your product or service creation, that connects all of the traditional silos into a significant event for each member of your audience. In taking this approach, you create experiences that provide the most satisfying outcome possible for your audience and result in the highest benefit for the organization, regardless of its for-profit or nonprofit directive.

In my consulting work, I often hear an organization express its desire to create an outstanding experience.

The organization may agree that the experience is important, even critical, but it often gets the details wrong. Why is that?

Instead of starting with the experience journey, organizations start with the specifics of technology, content, or some other aspect of the business. It's backward thinking: you can't start with the implementation details and end up with a remarkable end-to-end experience. A mind shift is necessary. The *experience* must come first, designed as it unfolds over time for the audience, for both the definition of the product or service as well as in assessing its business success. The experience forms the foundation; then you can create the components to bring the experience to life in the right order, with the right connections and dependencies.

This thorough understanding will help you find the starting point of the experience; then you can move forward to determine

When you take a holistic look at how people react and would interact within a set of events at specific points in time, you are implementing Experience Thinking.

the specific components in your designs to build the end-to-end experience.

The Experience Thinking concept works equally well with products and services that are existing or new. Start by creating early, non-technically working versions of the experience, and involve the business stakeholders, the (potential) users, and customers in that process to learn, assess, and adjust. It's a fallacy that an actual

working product or service is needed in order to evaluate its potential for success.

Instead, create experiences fit for specific purposes, even if they are throwaway versions, that answer these questions: Will the experience suffice for users and customers? Will it deliver enough to meet the business goals? If the answer to both is yes, you can continue to fill out the other components that will also include technology and content.

Complete Design

In experience design, you want to create the entire experience. This means all products and services—everything in the environment. Of course, there's no such thing as "entire," but you can get close if you think like a filmmaker, one of the best examples of a true experience designer.

In creating a film, the filmmaker creates a complete world for the viewer. A good filmmaker uses the concepts of experience design to give the viewer the total package—sights, sounds, emotions, meaning, flow, intensity, and more. The film is even more experiential when the theater contributes additional elements such as moving chairs and 180-degree viewing angles, so the viewer becomes completely immersed in the moment.

If you can think like a filmmaker when building a product, a service, an app, a piece of hardware, or a space, you'll start to understand what the experience should consist of. What's the end-to-end experience of your product? Where will it live? How long will it be a part of someone's life? When you start thinking about the product from the experience side first, you learn the answers to all such questions, and your build has a much better chance of success. Filmmakers understand much of the experience that they are creating before hiring the first actor or booking the first location.

Similarly, office builders don't just jump in and start constructing a wall. There's a plan, created by the architect. The vision of the architect comes first, then the blueprint with calculations so that the building doesn't collapse, and then the building starts. A builder would never start erecting walls without first understanding what the final result will look like, based on the blueprint.

In product and service design, the experience is the blueprint. More mature industries are good examples, because they seem to have a better understanding of the role that experience plays. For example, car makers know that their customers don't necessarily care about technology or engineering. Every company in the automotive sector can build a car. It's not about the clutch, the brakes, or the engine— as long as they reliably work. It's all about the design and the experience, so car makers start designing their own blueprint. How does the car smell? How does it drive? How does the car door sound when it closes? How does the engine sound? How does it make you feel when you are sitting in the driver's seat? The driver experience is a key point of differentiation.

Creating a Film Experience

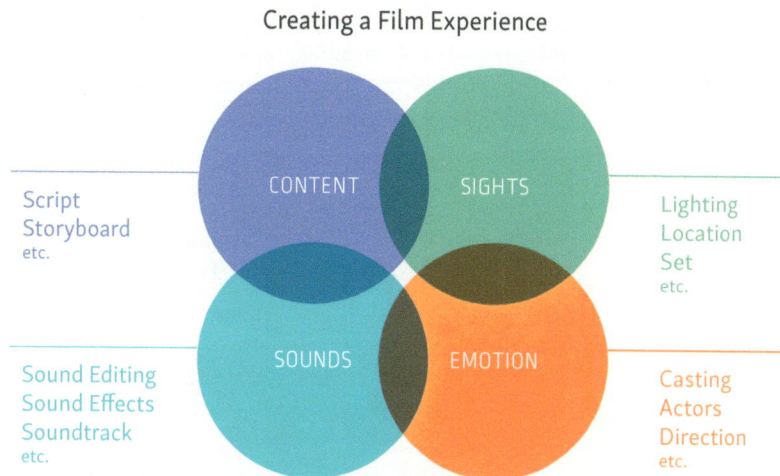

Script
Storyboard
etc.

CONTENT   SIGHTS

Lighting
Location
Set
etc.

Sound Editing
Sound Effects
Soundtrack
etc.

SOUNDS   EMOTION

Casting
Actors
Direction
etc.

Make sure you design for the complete environment. Don't rely only on a bottom-up approach where you start with the technology, functionality, and content, only to add the experience layer on top. Start with a top-down design, from an experiential viewpoint, and go from there. Both top-down and bottom-up design will need to happen, but start with top-down design for the best results.

The Balance of Design & Technology

The point of Experience Thinking is to get the necessary information and insight *before* you commit time and resources to building a product. Rather than evaluating the product after the fact, consider the risks early.

It's a little magical when you think about it: you are going to create the experience without actually building anything. In this way, you can evaluate the experience and know you are building the *right* thing. Ideal product solutions often lie somewhere between design and technology, and Experience Thinking can help you create the right mix.

When the focus is mainly on technology, you may end up with a functional product that is ultimately a failure. On the flip side, Experience Thinking can't be solely about design. The most beautifully designed and marketed product may still fail, because it's not about simply looking good—that would be art. You want to create a design that meets an audience need as well as a business need. If your product doesn't meet both needs, it will fail in the end or be replaced by something better, regardless of how stunning it is or how easy it is to use.

Consider the iPad. We were all wowed by the design and cool qualities at first, but tablet use is diminishing. Reality has kicked in, and the tablet doesn't add as much value as it once did, or as we once thought it did. Laptops have gotten smaller and phones have gotten larger, and the iPad is no longer meeting the needs of many users.

The key is balance. Apply Experience Thinking to make sure you give equal attention to the design, interaction, content, and functionality. When you validate and test the experience early with your audience, you will create a focused design that serves the right purpose.

Users want more than functionality; they want experiences.

Benefits of Experience Thinking

Experience Thinking includes a repeatable process, but most of all, it makes sense. It connects the dots along the customer's journey, connects the details, and drives the creation of remarkable experiences. Although improving the design of often-disjointed events experienced by your customer creates client loyalty and increases business success in the end, the benefits of designing the experience first can be found at every stage of your project.

EXPERIENCE THINKING ENHANCES GOOD ENGINEERING

Once you know what the experience is, you can build to fit it. Experience Thinking flips the process on its head and drives engineering, rather than the engineering driving the design.

By creating the experience first, you avoid the mental churn of trying to figure out what need the design will fulfill. There's no need for each decision maker to gaze into a crystal ball for options as they try to predict the future in incremental steps. Even when the options seem exhausted, they are probably wrong, outdated, or at least incomplete.

Decision makers need to assume that they are missing some requirements during the design process. Even if the CEO and engineers are experts in their field, the shortest way to get a successful end result is to understand the user, create early mock-ups, and test the design before committing significant resources to the building phase.

Additionally, this testing must be conducted with the only true expert—the user.

Follow a similar approach even if there is no product or service experience like yours yet on the market. After assessing the market potential, create designs and mock-ups of the anticipated experience, and test these concepts with potential customers and users. In the testing, look for early evidence to determine if the new product or service will fill a need, will be bought, and will be valued. This can all be accomplished without really building the product or delivering the service. This is a phase where design helps de-risk the business case, creating a validated Experience Case (XC) that complements the Business Case (BC) for a new initiative.

In many of the current approaches, the marketplace tests the experience. Then, the engineers begin an iterative fixing-and-adding pattern to the experience design. They work with their fingers crossed that the market will respond positively.

24

Through Experience Thinking, you can move that moment of success to the front of the process. Wouldn't you rather release a version that delivers the right experience in release one, or two at the latest? Wouldn't that make sense?

The argument is often that there is a need to go to market earlier in order to create revenue. This real or perceived need results in launching unfinished experiences that actually hurt market success. In hindsight, it may be unclear what went wrong. More often than not, however, unmet customer needs and a sub-par level of experience drift to the top as reasons for market failure. These things can be prevented by taking a harder look at what experience is going to fly, and committing engineering resources to building it. It's a sensible approach that all too often gets overruled by risky corner cutting.

EXPERIENCE THINKING IMPACTS BUSINESS & MARKETING STRATEGY

In order to implement a successful strategy and design for a new product, you have to understand your customers and your users. They can't be treated equally. Experience Thinking is a process to understand the unique needs of members of your audience at each stage of their journey so you can optimally design the experiences of each journey.

This means that customers—the people that buy, value, and benefit from your offering—need an experience that is tailored to exactly that. The experience must tell the customer why she should buy from you, what your value is, and what product benefits she will enjoy once she's handed over the cash. This is a distinct type of experience design that focuses on the customer.

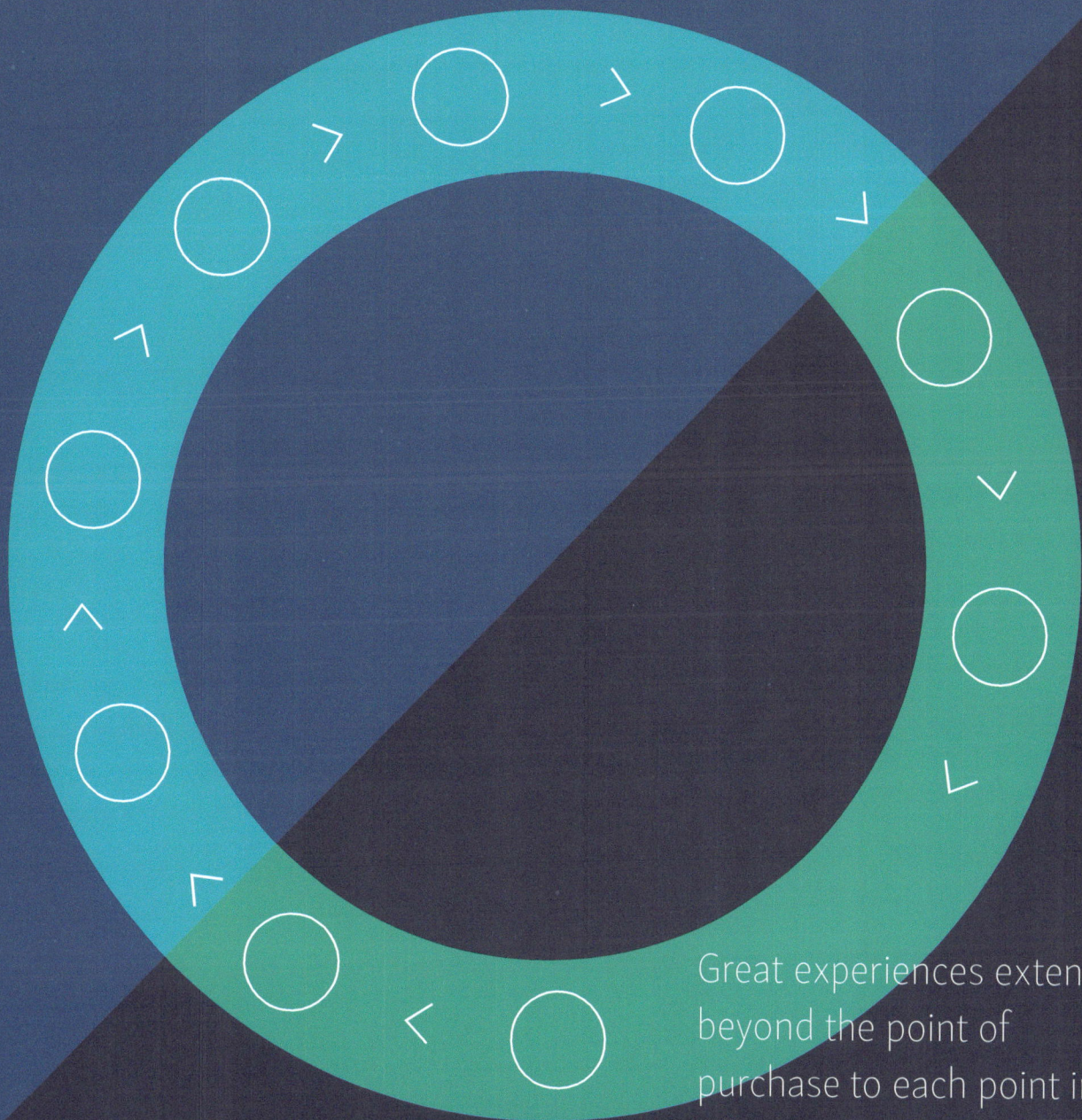

Great experiences extend beyond the point of purchase to each point in the experience lifecycle.

It all changes once she's bought a product, onboarded, or signed up for the service. In that moment, she changes from a customer to a user. The user's interest shifts to a focus on enjoying the benefits of the experience she's just bought, as well as finding out how it works and what it's like to use the product. The user gets immersed in the product/service experience and reaps the reward of a remarkably designed experience.

It is at this moment (and research supports this in no uncertain terms) that the satisfaction and delight in the brand or product starts to diminish. The customer high was the moment of purchase or onboarding, and nothing after that meets or exceeds that thrill. Why is that? What makes the customer experience so much better than the user experience? What is this sinking feeling that we endured a bait and switch where the company lured us in just to desert us at the shiny portal into their ecosystem?

This is where the holistic, end-to-end experience lifecycle saves the day. They have to keep delivering experiences that meet or exceed the customer experience before engaging, committing, or onboarding. For this reason, Experience Thinking is a powerful tool for any organization that wants to improve their delivery and innovate at the experience level, where it really matters.

Throughout the experience lifecycle, from customer to user to loyal client, organizations need to acquire new customers, but most of all, they need to keep their audience captured in their ecosystem. Successful companies do this by taking care of their audience in the customer experience phases, and by providing excellent experiences all the way down the product and service lifecycle.

Companies do themselves a disservice when the user experience is not up to the standard of the customer experience. When a user is unsatisfied post-purchase, they are less likely to make repeat purchases. However, when equal attention is paid to ease of use and other post-purchase phases, users will become loyal clients and return for more.

Apple is a company that created a user experience to rival all others. They have a great marketing team, but it's the ease of use and the high level of quality that keeps customers coming back. The value is embedded in the products. The great experience doesn't stop at the final sale; it continues from cradle to grave.

It's not enough to focus on only the business and profit side, or on just the engineering and product-building side, or on just marketing, or on just support. Put yourself in the shoes

If an organization wants to create loyal and vocal fans of their products and services who keep coming back, they have to extend the 'wow'.

of your customer, and make sure they can move seamlessly from one experience point to the next without losing interest.

EXPERIENCE THINKING JUSTIFIES INVESTMENTS IN PROCESS & PEOPLE

The strategic impact of Experience Thinking doesn't only reach the understanding and design aspects of product creation. It also plays an important role in bringing proof that the experience delivers to the business strategy. This proof is a critical business need in order to justify investments of time, money, and people. Without proof, we are merely assuming the experience will deliver success: a real-life, fingers-crossed approach. Yet those assumptions (and gut feel) are often the shaky foundation that many teams and organizations rely on. So we reason our way through what a customer or user would need, do, and experience, and we want to believe that it will work out.

The challenge lies in that when we design, we can only look at what users did in the past, which sometimes is a predictor of future behavior, but that gets increasingly tenuous the more disruptive the new product or service is. We simply don't know enough about the future customer or user behavior to assure success. We increase risk, something all organizations try to reduce.

So how do we de-risk our experience? In Experience Thinking, we move from the combination of reasoning, assumptions, and personal beliefs to reasoning, proof, and ultimately management buy-in.

Design de-risking happens when we take an unpolished experience, and we gather feedback (i.e., test results) from our audience. Then we iterate the unpolished experience, gather more feedback, and optimize further. Usually, two iterations lead to vastly reduced risk while balancing business constraints. The testing is another story.

Finding proof that the experience will deliver *before* we launch into the market is where this approach vastly de-risks the experience.

There are distinct differences between customers and users, and the testing is also different. Customer testing of the experience revolves around whether the person would buy the product. Does the customer see value? What is it about the product that is interesting to the customer? How can the product be marketed to address those answers?

The second level of testing is based on whether or not someone can actually use the product or service. Can they turn it on? Can they interact with the product in the

way it is intended? Can they complete the service onboarding process? These things are critical to the user's perception of the overall experience. Keep in mind that this testing is not about blindly following customer or user demands. You can't please everyone. Your goal is to test and validate, iterate, and ultimately deliver experiences that are usable and that meet a real need. The only way to get solid proof of the success of those differentiating features is to get as close as you can to the real experience early on and involve prospective customer and users.

Chapter 2

THINK YOU DON'T NEED AN EXPERIENCE STRATEGY?

Experience is ultimately what you deliver and what your audience lives through. If the overall experience isn't a good one, chances are you'll lose your customer or user to a competitor.

To win in today's hypercompetitive business environment, companies must research, design, strategize, and test their products and services before they launch. If you can engineer memorable product and service experiences, you will firmly position your organization in the hearts and minds of customers. Happy users become loyal clients, and loyal clients add to your bottom line.

Experiential elements are all connected. It's not just about technology, vision, or brand alone. Without an experience strategy in place that addresses every experience point, and connects them cohesively, you can't guarantee an overall positive experience for your customer or user.

Can you really afford to cut corners when designing the customer experience journey?

Why wouldn't you approach design from the perspective of Experience Thinking?

1,001 Reasons We Ignore the Opportunity

Experience Thinking is the holistic approach to experience design. Most organizations agree that the customer or citizen comes first, yet they don't apply the concepts that create demonstrable value. The reasons for ignoring these opportunities are numerous and often unfounded.

"It Will Add Additional Costs and Extend Our Timeline"

A common misconception about designing for the experience first is that it's more expensive than traditional design processes. While there are up-front costs with experience design, building the wrong thing is much more expensive in the end. Often, the greatest expense is the failure. It costs much more to build something that nobody wants, nobody buys, and nobody uses.

In reality, experience design is not a huge expense, because you get the information you need before you produce anything. Getting early feedback on functionality cuts down on the expensive journey of building the wrong thing, as well as the endless arguing in a vacuum about features and functions.

A common cause of time and cost overruns is changes in requirements throughout the project. It's easy for clients and stakeholders to change their minds about what they want because they really have no idea what the customer will value. Is it cost-effective to spend millions on the gut feeling of an executive or one lead customer? Can one data point that is not of a target user of the product be enough proof of what the product should be?

Experience design doesn't extend timelines or processes. There are fewer changes when your requirements are of higher quality at the start of your project. The rest is quite predictable. Up-front planning saves time and expense down the road.

"No One Knows Our Market Better Than We Do"

Some organizations are reluctant to apply a different design process to help them improve their own product's experience. They think that no one could know their market, product, or user better than they do. These executives are missing the point. It's a fallacy that the experience designer has to be an up-front domain expert in the particular market.

Regardless of the product or category it belongs to, the process of involving customers and users to understand the experience and validate use is similar, even if the specific tools and inquiries vary. It's actually often preferred to start without preconceived notions of your customers and users. You can't assume you know what kind of functionality should be in a product experience simply because you've been in business awhile.

User needs evolve over time, and static assumptions rarely lead to sustained success.

You may think you know your users, but the way they use products can change very quickly. For example, *mobile* may be defined as using "on the go," but what if your app is most frequently used on the couch? It may not be that "mobile" at all.

Users can be a fickle group. You can't know what your users want or need, or how they'll behave, unless you ask them in current time. Don't make assumptions based on what you've always known to be true. When you rely on such assumptions, you're basing your requirements on your own anecdote-based opinions, not on the observed behavior of your real audience today.

"We Don't Want Outside Interference in Our Business"

If you're hesitant to work with external consultants, there's another way: make experience design a part of your core business! Just like you hire in-house engineering, human resources, finance, sales, or marketing professionals, hire experience designers, user researchers, and experience testers as part of your core team.

An in-house research and design team helps you determine your requirements for a project before expending resources. For example, instead of having five coders on staff before you even know what needs coding, understand and validate concept designs first. You will have a better sense of what you need.

Before you hire more people that can build stuff, decide what kind of company you are. What is your key differentiator? More often than not, "ease of use" or "an effortless experience" is part of your top-three unique selling points. Before outsourcing the actual experience design work, consider hiring not only the designers and researchers, but also higher-level strategic thinkers who can work with management to discover the right products. You want to build value, and value is expressed through the experience. To consistently build great experiences, you will need a robust experience design process and strategy to keep delivering excellence.

"We'd Rather Be Reactive"

Another reason some organizations don't immediately implement Experience Thinking is because they're stuck in a reactive mentality. They assume they know their customers and will be able to change in appropriate ways as the need arises. There's nothing inherently wrong with this attitude, but wouldn't you rather work more efficiently?

Why *react* to unforeseen complaints when experience design can help you be *proactive*? Wouldn't you rather anticipate and solve most problems before they occur?

The prevailing approach in some digital product cases seems to be to launch and make fixes later. This may even be after the fourth release of the product or service! There are ever-changing business names for these processes that make an organization feel better about the state of its operations. Though there may be occasions when doing the "minimum viable product" launch or starting "lean" may work, the concepts in Experience Thinking eliminate much of the time and money required to build, get feedback, fix, and repeat.

In more mature industries, design flaws can result in wide-scale product recalls (cars), worker accidents (building), and even deaths (airplanes). The companies in these markets see the need to get the product experience quality right *before* launch.

The consequences are simply too high. When is the digital industry going to catch up?

"Experience Variables Are Too Difficult to Measure"

Good experience design isn't magic; it's a scientific approach from the perspective of the customer. Although experiences are not easily measured, there are quantifiable data that you can rely on when you compare the reactions of customers. For example, specific measures might include customer preference of the new design over the old one (emotion), giving the right information to the customer (usefulness), or the amount of time it takes to get the requested information. Another metric is whether or not the customer would recommend the product or service to another based on the experience.

On the commerce side, you simply look at your business success. Did the customer buy or not? What were the conversion rates, and where did changes occur in the sales funnel?

It's equally as easy to quantify success in "use." Again, it's a matter of testing. Give users the product, and see if they can successfully use it in the way it's intended to be used. When you watch and record the interaction of the user with the product, service, or app, you get a very clear "yes or no" answer to the question of whether your experience design is successful. If your client can't complete the task, sign up, or make the transaction in a reasonable time with little help or training, you know you have issues.

Benchmarking on the experience side, not just the technology side, is another way to make sure you are creating the best possible user experience. First test, then redesign to make the product better than it previously tested, and repeat. Designers can try to improve their build in ways to

make the percentage of task completion better and the satisfaction level higher.

Key experience metrics include market and user research through surveys, focus groups, interviews, or observation. How do users behave? How do customers perceive? When the experience is good and people can use the product easily, they're happier and more engaged. When consumers and users are happier, companies will see a direct correlation in advocacy, in sales, and ultimately in business impact.

Are You Ready to Embrace Change?

Change is a constant in business. When you change your process or design, there's always a risk. But if you do it in the right way, the risk will be outweighed by the immense benefits to your customer, to your user, and to your bottom line.

Experience Thinking is logical and holistic. Embrace it, and you will deliver ongoing value in tune with your audience's needs and desires.

PART TWO

About
Experience Thinking

Chapter 3
───────────

STRUCTURE: PEOPLE, BUSINESS, PROCESS & TECHNOLOGY

Underlying every awesome experience is an organizational structure that creates it. Four areas tightly align to deliver experiences successfully: people, business, process, and technology. Each area must be aligned to deliver.

TECHNOLOGY

PROCESS

BUSINESS

PEOPLE

Too many organizations are only partly aligned, and their delivered experience value suffers. They may have a great business model, but no good technology to support the experience, or the people may be on board, but the software development process doesn't allow for rapid experimentation and ongoing improvements. For the alignment to work well, each organizational area must be aware and recognize that the experience is the future differentiator.

People, Competence, & Culture

The experience starts with people. It always has and it always will. Hire the right competencies, train existing staff, and create a supportive culture. All of these elements are foundational to long-term and widespread adoption of realizing that the experience comes first and brings organizational success. The rest flows from here.

Many failed initiatives are the result of underinvestment into the human element of experience design. Companies often underspend and hope that staff and stakeholders will magically see the light on their own and start adopting Experience Thinking with wild abandon. It doesn't work like that. It takes deliberate action, planned communication, training, on-the-job support, and ongoing monitoring to keep the human engaged and focused on the goal: creating awesome experiences for your ecosystem by putting the experience first.

Driving Business Models

The business model defines how an organization makes money or meets its mandate in a sustained way. It's also the thing that makes or ultimately breaks any business initiative.

In some cases, companies become wed to their amazing business model so much that they assume it *has* to be successful. More commonly, however, the business model is driving and propelling the offering, but it's rarely the only reason that it's successful.

As soon as companies talk about the customer or user experience, everything gets fuzzy. Lofty statements are made that people will flock to the product or service because of the experience. How you create that experience, however, and how you deliver its awesomeness remains vague. This is because the business model drives,

Sustained success needs a well-executed, complete, and robust experience on top of a great business model to make it sing.

not steers. Although it addresses the anticipated impact to the business, it stops there. It doesn't tell you how to *create* the experience.

Superior Design Processes

Internal processes are a constant source of interest and frustration for all organizations. There's always something to improve, change, align, and discard. No process escapes the critical eye of its stakeholders and the people executing it. Whether it's in operations, finance, human resources, or sales, there are opportunities to become better almost every day.

In theory, this means that you would expect a similar kind of scrutiny in how you design the experiences you deliver. Surprisingly, this doesn't happen enough. Many organizations still have a low maturity in experience design and research processes. They apply ad hoc, per project approaches that are sometimes of high quality. Unfortunately, the next project falls back to utter mediocrity because no framework is in place to repeat best-in-class design steps and processes.

Most businesses know how to introduce and repeat superior processes in an organization. At this point, however, experience design seems to be the exception because the prevalent thinking is that experience design and research is "special" and doesn't need to follow regular business methods. Nothing could be further from the truth. The experience design field needs to mature and see itself as a part of a regular business (like finance, human resources, operations, etc.) and adopt the organizational structures that go with it.

Viewing design and research processes as part of the core business is the only way to be both recognized by the other parts of the business as a full member of the family, and get the organizational support to be successful in a sustained way.

Enabling Technologies

In addition to people, the business model, and internal processes, the essential fourth element is the technology that allows delivery of the experiences. Technology in this context is broadly defined to include hardware, software, and data, and is both an enabler for new and exciting experiences as well as a detriment to innovation. As soon as technology is used in an experience, it's outdated because it becomes the old way of doing things, now waiting to be overtaken by the next new thing.

For this reason, technology can never be seen as the main goal. Of the four structural elements in the experience thinking framework, technology is the most fluid, the most interchangeable, and therefore the highest

risk. Experiences based on mostly people, business models, and processes are more stable because technology is continually

Organizations align and incorporate all of the structural pieces to deliver the experience.

switched out for something newer (i.e., mainframe to desktop app to web to mobile).

At the foundational stage, technology is the fourth element that the business must consider as they start to ask questions like these: Now what? How is this product or service going to work? What is the experience going to be like?

What About the End-to-End Experience?

In answer, the business decides they need a product with considerable content, or media, or a brand, or a service, or maybe all four. Without a framework of how to design the experience, this process is overwhelming, and each designed step in the experience is approached ad hoc, stumbling along as more is learned about what the experience lifecycle is going to be like.

Instead of designing for a series of interconnected experiences in the customer's journey, organizations design experience islands that are fragmented pieces of the whole. They've forgotten to take into account an essential element. In the adrenaline-filled rush to create the basis of a new initiative, the "big idea" often takes center stage. There's

nothing wrong with putting focus on the profitable business model, the amazing technology, or immersive engagement, but they all must be seamlessly connected if you want to deliver to the audience's needs.

While an organization's secret sauce may actually turn out to be the business model or the enabling technology, there's a third key differentiator—the end-to-end experience. If your organization has any interaction with customers or users, the experience must also be addressed in these initial stages of product design. The brilliance of the model and technologies will not be able to compensate for deficiencies in the overall experience, which must move from initial awareness, through to recycling the product or canceling the service—end-to-end.

The audience reacts to their experience with the organization, regardless of whether that experience was intentionally created with them in mind. Even if your technology is cutting-edge, the user won't care as long as the desired result occurs when they touch the screen. They press a key on the keyboard; and their experience, not your technology, becomes the most important aspect of the interaction. All of the databases underneath and the wonderful technology choices you've made are important, but ultimately they're less important when the user is in the midst of experiencing what you've created.

The experience is not something that can be added on later in the process. Instead, it's one of the three big initial questions that must be answered as an organization contemplates an initiative: What's the business model? What's the technology? What's the experience? Create a balance, and include the experience in this conversation to build not only the business case, but also the experience case for your offering.

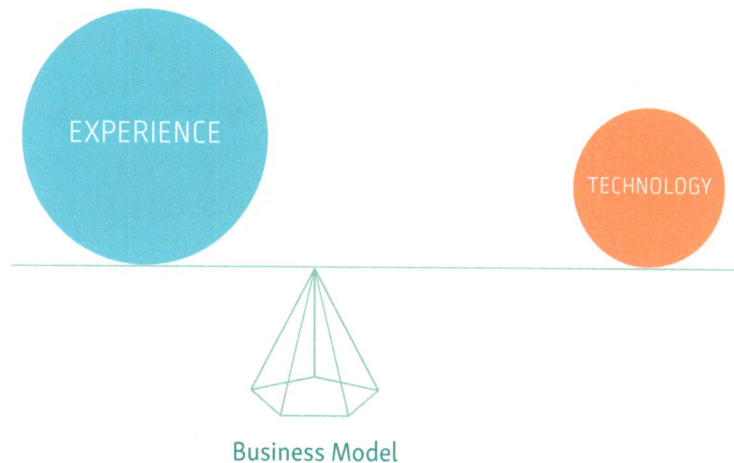

EXPERIENCE

TECHNOLOGY

Business Model

Chapter 4

THE EXPERIENCE THINKING FRAMEWORK

Experience Thinking is a design approach that helps you create your audience's journeys and their connected end-to-end experiences following the organization's business model and technologies.

The experience is not created in a vacuum or as an afterthought. An organization has to find ways to intentionally transform the people, processes, their business model, and technology into something amazing for their audience.

Two distinct inquiries are necessary if you want to create the best experience for your audience. The first occurs as you use the experience lifecycle (see Part Three) as a tool to understand the experience from an external, audience perspective.

As you investigate what your audience encounters, you have a better understanding of what you lack, and what might make the experience more cohesive.

The second inquiry is internal, within the organization. Once you know what needs to be done from the external point of view, you start investigating the best ways to make it happen.

There are four key experiences that need to be created to improve and innovate customer and user journeys: Brand, Product, Content and Service.

Four Experience Quadrants

Each of these experience quadrants involves a somewhat distinct research and design process with its own set of goals, techniques, and outcomes. Often, all four must be researched and designed in close collaboration, but distinctly, in your organization.

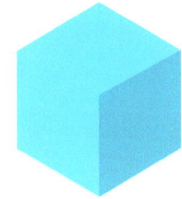

Service

Content

Product

Brand

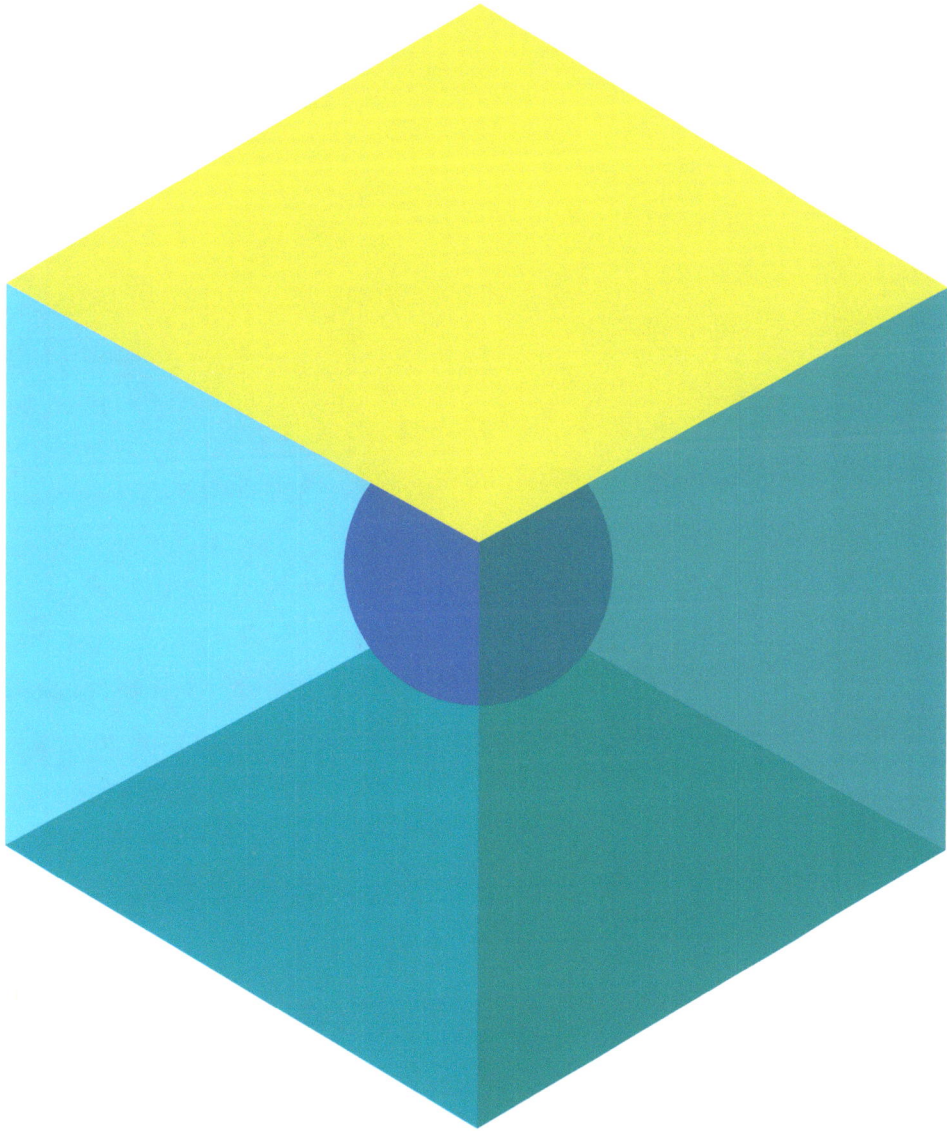

The point of using these experience quadrants for creating the overall experience is to delineate the specific areas where each design element is needed. Design conversations get convoluted very quickly unless you precisely narrow your focus. For example, if you decided to build an app, you might start with the business model. In the same conversation, you might discuss the app's product design and its ease of use. There may be other elements as well, such as a related service, the different customer and user experiences, the functionality, and the content displayed in the app.

Instead of dealing with such a tangled web in broad strokes, it's better to engage the four experiences to separate the design challenges and simplify the process. In the following chapters, we'll take a close look at how each of these experience quadrants can be optimized.

We will begin with *brand*, which is the foundational element of any experience. If you don't have a brand defined, the other experience designs will struggle to become cohesive and connected.

After brand, the focus is on *content* and *product* experience design. These design processes go hand in hand because many "things," such as mobile apps, software, web applications, and websites, have both content and product aspects that need their own distinct design process.

The final component to be addressed is *service* experience design. In service design, we often see a combination of product and content that is deliberately designed into a service offering that supports specific parts of an experience journey and/or lifecycle.

Let's start with brand.

Narrow your focus so you can have the right conversation at the right time.

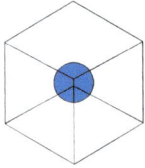

Chapter 5

EXPERIENCE THINKING FOR BRAND

One definition of "branding" is the way an organization chooses to communicate its values, differentiators, and image in the audience's mind. Defining a strong brand requires a process of discovery to define your vision and design for the qualities you want associated with your organization.

Your brand is also an aggregation of all the experiences during the experience lifecycle. This means your brand becomes not just what you want it to be, but also what your audience thinks and feels about you over time.

Branding includes the *brand promise*—what you are committing to deliver to your audience. Once you have a clear brand promise, it will guide your brand design down the road.

In the beginning, an organization's brand is not much more than something to market around. It's still just an empty assurance from the organization that the product or service will do what you say it will. Once your audience *experiences* the brand and becomes a part of the ecosystem of the organization, your brand starts to carry more weight. The more consistently you deliver on your brand promise, the more loyal your audience will become.

Emotional reactions will fluctuate depending on the gut feelings of the customer during every microinteraction. Even in the face of the emotional ups and downs, the cumulative reaction will be positive if the brand promise is continually kept. It's only in the long-term experience and use of the offering that a brand is fully formed and becomes difficult to change.

Branding goes beyond the tangible. A brand is not just defined by its logo, name, color scheme, or tagline; instead, it's all about the emotion that's created as your promise is manifested in numerous customer and user experiences.

Although organizations often try to jump too quickly from the brand promise to the brand experience in one shot, it can't happen overnight. Just because you promise great service doesn't mean great service is somehow baked into the experience.

Your brand must be built. Great service isn't created by a new package or value proposition. Concrete customer experiences, followed by real user experiences, must manifest and support your promise over time.

There's a reason we all think of quality when we hear Mercedes, and safety when we hear Volvo. It's not only because Mercedes has a great marketing team that used the right colors and messages to convey that they are a well-built brand (although that didn't hurt). Instead, they decided on their brand promise, and they created an experience to reflect it, even down to the solid sound of the doors closing. Mercedes, as well as Volvo, earned their respected reputation by consistently delivering on their promises.

Their brand experience reflects the quality and safety they continually provide.

Today, it's very easy for your audience to express their opinion about your organization. This can work for you or against you. Bad news and negative comments travel very quickly, but positive opinions will also be shared. Tell customers what to expect from you, then deliver on your promise consistently, and you will realize the benefits. The more often what you say you are through the brand promise matches what your audiences say you are through the brand experience, the stronger your brand will be. So how do you plan for the creation of the brand experience?

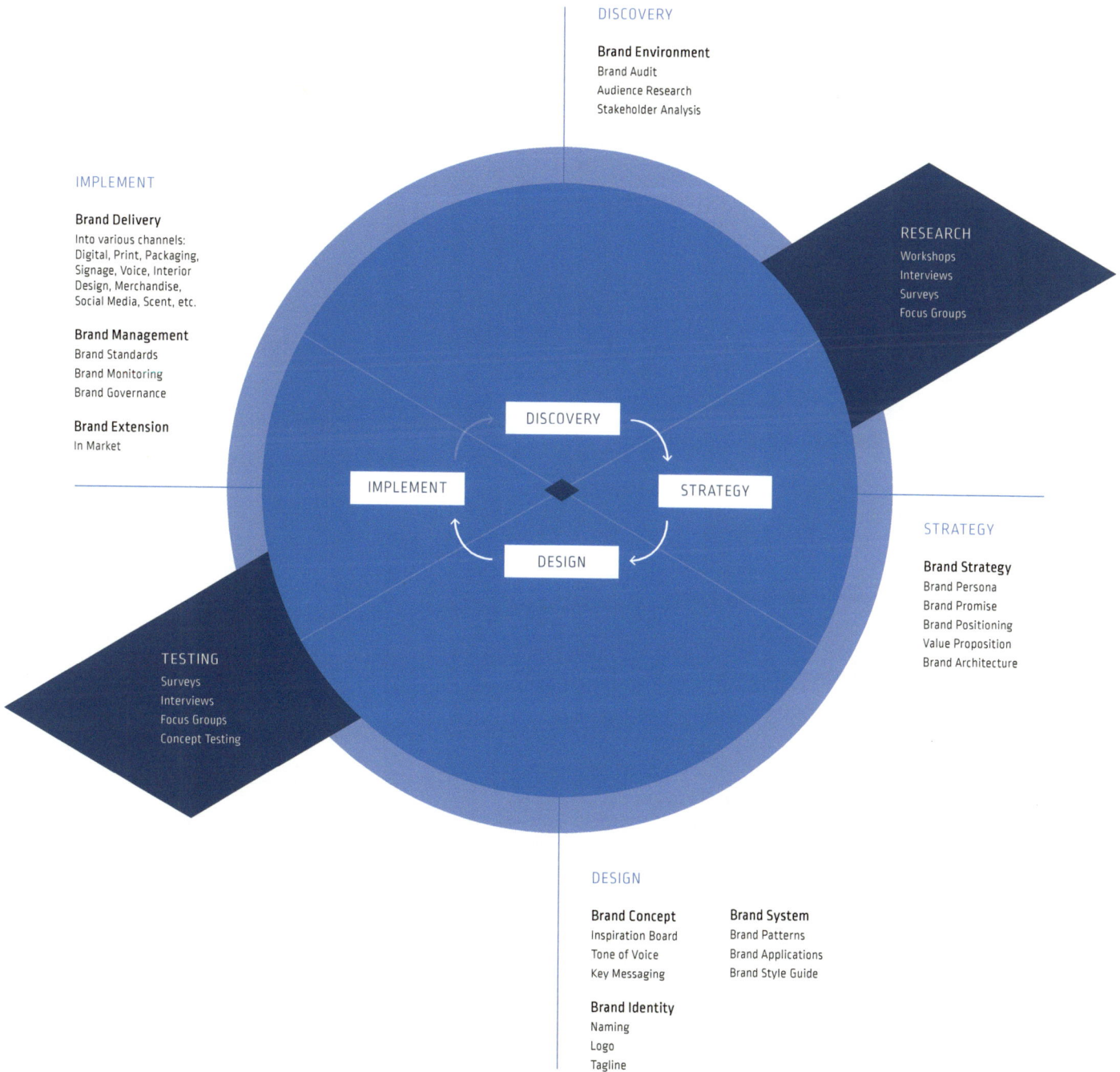

BRAND

DISCOVERY

Brand Environment
Brand Audit
Audience Research
Stakeholder Analysis

IMPLEMENT

Brand Delivery
Into various channels:
Digital, Print, Packaging,
Signage, Voice, Interior
Design, Merchandise,
Social Media, Scent, etc.

Brand Management
Brand Standards
Brand Monitoring
Brand Governance

Brand Extension
In Market

RESEARCH
Workshops
Interviews
Surveys
Focus Groups

STRATEGY

Brand Strategy
Brand Persona
Brand Promise
Brand Positioning
Value Proposition
Brand Architecture

TESTING
Surveys
Interviews
Focus Groups
Concept Testing

DISCOVERY

STRATEGY

IMPLEMENT

DESIGN

DESIGN

Brand Concept
Inspiration Board
Tone of Voice
Key Messaging

Brand Identity
Naming
Logo
Tagline

Brand System
Brand Patterns
Brand Applications
Brand Style Guide

Experience Thinking Process

Brand Experience In Ten Steps

The brand experience process has four main phases: discovery, strategy, design, and implement. Brand experience design is a foundational activity that builds on the organizational structure and culture to make a meaningful connection with audiences. Brand experiences should precede product, content and service experience creation.

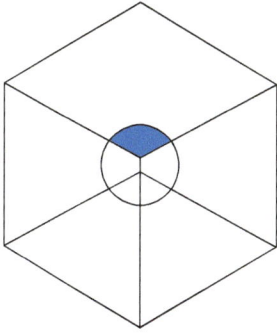

Discovery Phase

BRAND ENVIRONMENT

The work and outcomes of the brand experience process are foundational for content, product, and service experiences. All of these experiences need to be embedded in the brand in order to position them for the audience. Sometimes it's in a direct sense, and other times it's through a gentle nudge to guide them. In any case, when the brand experience design process begins in the discovery phase, the outside world where the brand is going to live is initially examined, prodded, and unearthed to thoroughly capture the future brand environment. In this step, you need to understand three elements that respectively look inward, outward, and sideways.

The future brand (totally new or refreshed from an existing brand) will have an audience for which it was created. Use **audience research**, through a combination of surveys, interviews, and prior customer research, to capture your preliminary understanding of the customers, users, and other types of audience segments that the brand will serve.

This research is expanded by an analysis of everything else that's out there in the market. Researching similar offerings and the brands that go with them will give you a great understanding of the competitive landscape that our future brand will need to compete and coexist with. It's part of the **brand audit** that also includes analysis of industry reports, a determination of the brand's (potential) effectiveness, and awareness and comparison of brands in similar and quite different markets with similar underlying market dynamics. This will give you an excellent appreciation of where your new or refreshed brand fits within the current brand landscape.

After looking outward and sideways, the understanding of both the audience and the competition provides great input to now look inward and capture the views and needs of internal stakeholders. The best way to do this is by conducting a **stakeholder analysis** inside the organization. Through workshops, interviews, and surveys, you will discover the perceptions and brand requirements of management, lines of business, specific departments, and other key individuals within the organization. When combined with the audience research and competitive insights, a well-rounded capture of the brand environment is created that sets you up for the next phase: brand strategy.

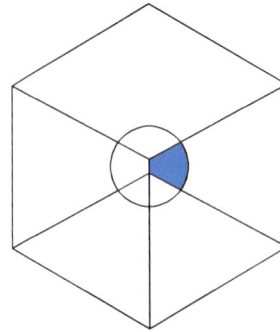

Strategy Phase

BRAND STRATEGY

In this strategy phase, you will work toward creating and capturing the requirements and vision of the new brand. Each activity in this step helps to further flesh out the brand strategy, which is the result of this phase.

The first activity is based on the discovery activities to date and allows you to build out a **brand persona**. This persona is a set of unique attributes or characteristics that capture the brand through human traits. Similar to a customer or user persona, you are creating a "stand in" of the brand with human values, traits, perceptions, and a description as if the brand were an actual human being with a family, background, demographics, and so on. The persona can be outgoing, introverted, flexible, stylish, jaded, or have swagger. You get the idea. Research and persona testing is needed to create a brand persona that truly becomes the "spokesperson" for your future brand.

Another important element in brand strategy is the creation of your **brand promise**, or what you promise to your audience. It's the unique benefit or essence of your offering that you deliver to your audience, again and again. You keep the promise so consistently over time that your audience relies on you to deliver on it, and starts to identify you with it. An example of an effective brand promise is Volvo. When you think Volvo, you think safety.

The brand promise can't be hyperbole. It's aspirational because it is the core of what you deliver to your audience. The promise

defines you as an organization and often goes *beyond* individual products or services.

Forming the brand promise is part art and part science. Workshops and creative sessions may help you define your brand promise, but sometimes it will come from a conversation by the stakeholders in a different meeting, even at the watercooler.

After the persona and promise, the third step broadens the emotional view on the brand. By creating a **brand positioning**, you aim to define how people feel about your brand: the emotions, associations, and perceptions your audience has when confronted with your brand. The brand position should lead the audience to realize how you're different from others and that what you're offering will help them particularly. This is often captured in a brief statement, the brand position statement.

The brand position statement is usually too dense to concretely guide the brand design, so we need to unpack the promise and articulate more specifics about it. You do this in the **value proposition** where you capture not only what the overall benefit of your offering is, but also *what* the specific offering is, *who* in your audience(s) would exactly benefit, and *how* your offering is different from the competition. These three questions are then asked through two different lenses to identify emotional values (feel) and rational values (think).

Allow for brainstorming, workshops, testing with audiences, and revisiting what you have. It should take several iterations to get to an effective value proposition.

Once you have created the brand persona, brand promise, brand positioning, and value

proposition, it is possible to move to the fifth activity necessary to create your overall brand strategy. In this activity, you define or redefine the overall structure or architecture of the new brand. Start by defining where and how your new brand relates to existing brands within the organization. In this **brand architecture** activity, determine how the new brand, associated value proposition, and brand promise should relate to your other brands, or your brand portfolio. Determine how to approach the brand. For example, should the offerings fall under one brand name? Or should the offerings be branded individually? Or is it a hybrid approach of the previous two?

Whichever brand architecture is chosen, the purpose is to align your business strategy with the brand strategy. How do they fit with your growth plans? Exploring and defining these brand relationships up front avoids many costly consequences down the road.

Understanding: Brand Research

In this process, both discovery and strategy phases can benefit from people research techniques to reach insights and check brand experience assumptions of the marketplace. Brand strategy is initially driven from within the organization. It's choosing who you want to be, and then checking the marketplace to see if there is an opening for your brand. There have been monumental brand failures because brand design projects haven't learned to let the customer audience into the design process. If you don't check in with your target audience while you're designing your brand, you will likely find some unpleasant surprises at launch.

The nature of brand research is initially to have internal stakeholders participate and articulate their goals. It's not always straightforward due to the abstract nature of branding that includes elements of communication, multichannel design, and aspirational messaging that both reflect and lead organizations and product teams. The use of **workshops**, **interviews**, and **focus groups** makes sense in these cases and successfully captures conceptual thinking in meaningful statements that can be used in design.

The goals, ideas, concepts, value statements, and positioning must be validated. Use interviews or focus groups to get deeper insight into what your audience perceives as matching your brand strategy. Do they identify with the brand? What do they think of the new brand in relation to your existing products and services?

Key brand research techniques include interviews, workshops, focus groups, panels, and online **survey** approaches.

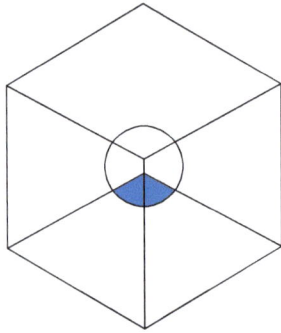

Design Phase

BRAND CONCEPT

With a brand strategy that captures clear requirements, the initial design aspects of the brand can be addressed. In this design phase, start to define the brand concept as a "response" to the brand positioning statement, promise, persona, value proposition, and architecture. The goal of this design step is to create a brand concept that takes the insights and direction of the strategy phase and combines them with creative thinking to address the business challenge.

To create a great brand concept, the concept design work includes creation of an **inspiration board**—a collage of images, materials, colors, and photos that start to reflect the intended emotion of the brand. The board looks accidental and unfinished, and that is intentional. The imagery and other elements on the board will show roughly where the brand concept thinking is headed. There will be many opportunities to explore further. The board works well as a communication tool that can easily be shared with business stakeholders to provide tangible participation in the design process.

The concept step also involves a deeper dive into what the brand will "sound" like. Exploring the **tone of voice** is critical in creating concepts that follow from the brand strategy. In any brand concept, there will be written messaging and statements. Developing an appropriate tone of voice is not just what you say, but how you say it.

Successfully capturing the brand persona through words will be one part of the brand concept. You can choose the language in your brand concept to be formal, casual, passionate, friendly, witty, or professional—just to name a few. You might even choose a deliberate combination of these voices.

Once you know the brand's tone, you have to decide exactly what you'd want to communicate to the audience. This is your **key messaging**, and it's explored with each different brand concept. The focus of a key message is to convey succinctly what your audience needs to hear about the value of the offering, the differentiators, and why they should choose you. The key messages are an important part of the brand and

subsequent marketing initiatives. The brand concepts incorporate the key messages.

The result of this step is one or more brand concepts. Each will be tested with both the target audience and key internal stakeholders to further iterate, refine, and select the brand concept to go forward with into the next phase.

BRAND IDENTITY

The second step in the brand design phase is developing the concept into a fully worked-out brand identity. This is the foundational piece that other brand expressions will be built upon. This step is often equated to brand design, but it is actually its own unique moment in the brand design process.

The first action to get to a brand identity is **brand naming**. The logo and the tagline (to a degree) are layers on top of the brand name. For example, the name can be descriptive—a thing, an acronym, a made-up word, or an alternative spelling to create a name that fits.

Many other types of naming are possible and usually benefit from initial workshops with the brand concept, competitive analysis, and brand strategy. Use these workshops to get input to generate naming ideas. Then, reduce the creative team to one or two people to continue to generate alternatives that will fit the brand strategy.

The reduction of the list of good naming candidates is done with the smallest possible team of stakeholders. Part of the list-reduction process can be testing of good naming candidates with audiences and outside stakeholders. Test for their stickiness, expression, and uniqueness among other characteristics. Use the testing results as input, not as an approach to make a final decision. *Boaty McBoatface* is a good example of a survey-based naming project gone wrong because the decision was left to the masses. Ultimately, stakeholders should make the final decision; and it will pay you to keep the decision-making group contained.

With the naming out of the way, you can design a **logo**. The logo is often a symbol of the whole organization, product, or even person. A logo is part of the brand, but it should not be considered the whole brand. There are many aspects to a logo: color, words (the company/product name), and a visual symbol.

The logo is foundational to the brand. It's an essential element that drives recognition and consistency in the company and acts as an outward communication to its audience. The logo design should strive to be distinctive, memorable, and timeless. As with naming, few stakeholders are needed to decide on the logo that will reflect both the brand strategy and, by extension, the business strategy. If desired, logo variations can be tested with other stakeholders and members of your target audience, but it's not always necessary.

The name and logo elements in a brand are often, but not always, joined by a **tagline.** This is a brief description that is associated with the brand, product, or service. A tagline is also simple and memorable. It's intended to present the benefit of the product or service in the minds of the audience. The tagline is the one element that potentially changes more often than the other two identity elements, logo and name. Taglines are often tested with audiences to see if they resonate, and if there is an overall effectiveness of meeting the brand strategy goals.

BRAND SYSTEM

With the identity designed, you can now create a brand system. This system is an extension and expansion of the brand identity. It includes not only the naming, logo, and tagline, but also brand concept elements such as tone of voice, key messaging, expanded typography, a palette of primary and secondary colors, and other brand elements that will be used in connection with the brand identity.

As part of the brand system, you need to design a library of **brand patterns**. These patterns are designs that may combine any number of identity elements, as well as other elements. For example, a brand pattern might show how the logo works when applied to a product, in a space, or on a website. It expands on the design of the singular logo, colors, or name and shows how these elements would appear in larger and different contexts. Where and how would the logo appear on clothing, on a product, or on the door to the office? Would it be in color or grayscale? Would a pen have both the name and the logo? What does it look like if we have the name, logo, and tagline altogether? These may seem like small decisions with insignificant impact, but as a whole, they can influence the overall brand perception positively or negatively. The brand patterns don't flesh out complete situations. Instead, they are meant to be an interim step to apply the brand identity and other elements in a consistent way, across mostly new and unknown circumstances.

If you know where the brand will be used in greater detail, you can design and capture a set of **brand applications**. They are expressions of the brand that are well defined and widely used in the organization. Examples are business cards, PowerPoint presentations, stationery, websites, staff uniforms, packaging, marketing campaigns, ads, video communications, billboards, and physical office locations. Brand applications may also include how employees speak to customers, how to answer the phone, or how to behave in traffic while driving the company truck. The brand application list can be quite extensive. When the organization has the brand applications defined and designed, they can decide on making a brand application guide, which is meant to be a suggestion for best practices, or a brand application standard, which is understood to be the definitive way things are done.

The brand identity results, brand patterns, and brand applications will be captured in a **brand style guide** (or even a standard). The guide is a document (or intranet site) that will support the creation of new experiences that need to follow the corporate brand style in some manner. It's a rich resource for designers and other stakeholders to follow in order to design consistent brand experiences.

Often, brand style guides focus on the core brand elements (logo use, name use, and print collateral). There are also many other style guides that can and should be created such as a web style guide, (technical) writing style guide, blogging style guide, software application or product style guide, social media style guide, interior design style guide, customer service style guide, and phone style guide. These are all examples where a connected and consistent brand experience will enhance the value of the brand, not only through a name, color, and logo.

Testing: Validating the Brand

If you want to test the brand identity (logo, name, tagline) and brand system (patterns, applications) with your target audience, this testing will follow the similar approach of brand **concept testing**. Test for qualities such as distinctiveness, memorability, visceral response, and first impressions.

Common testing methods are **focus groups**, **surveys**, and **interviews**. Research in groups, remote and in-person, will provide insights into what the brand means for its audience and how it aligns with their expectations, attitudes, and perceptions. When testing is done early enough, the feedback can be used to iterate the designs further and improve them with these insights.

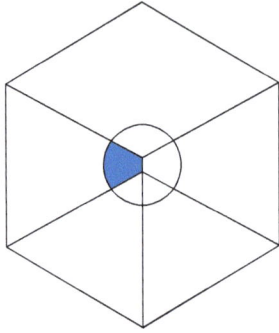

Implement Phase

BRAND DELIVERY

The finishing phase in brand experience design is when the brand system, its applications, and its components are implemented. In the first step, brand delivery, you deliver the brand in its multitude of applications. The brand system becomes a reality through various projects, programs, events, campaigns, customer service processes, and other customer-facing interactions where the brand will help deliver the optimal experience to your audience. These projects may be substantive and complex, especially when

more than one brand application needs to work together (i.e., a mobile app based on an online marketing campaign leading up to multi-city events in different venues).

The brand experience will shape many outreach initiatives of the organization, and the brand will reach the audience through a combination of product, content, and service experiences. Ultimately, the overall experience that the audience will undergo is from all four experience quadrants.

BRAND MANAGEMENT

The second and ongoing step in the implementation phase is management of the brand throughout the organization and distinct experience lifecycles. This is often a role of an individual or a team that safeguards the appropriate application of the brand in all experiences that the organization delivers. This is accomplished through several activities.

The first activity builds on the brand style guides created in the design phase. At some point in the maturity of the organization, the worth of a valuable brand will be recognized and consistently applied across experiences. **Brand standards** elevate this notion and makes the brand system something that must be adhered to, instead of being seen as an optional guide.

Each expression of the brand will be evaluated against the brand standard and either approved or turned back for redesign. This brings the brand Experience Thinking up to par with other elements in the organizational structure such as financial reporting requirements, procurement processes, HR hiring and firing procedures, and operational process directives, including safety standards that also must be adhered to. Brand system application joins the list of elements that must be done right because the business impact can be severe.

Having the standards in place requires continuous **brand monitoring** to have your internal audience observe the brand standard. As designs are created, you can have a check-in step and monitor at the process level during that phase. Monitoring can also be at the in-market level where you check what's out there and if it follows the brand standard, resulting in corrective action. These preventative and curative approaches need to work side by side to implement a brand standard that remains well regarded and elevates the organizational brand perception.

Both brand monitoring and creating and following the brand standard must be anchored in a defined and shared **brand governance** model. This model captures the responsibilities of each stakeholder.

You must know who has what kind of brand authority, where in the organization the decisions are made regarding brand design and brand standards, and in what manner the brand system is applied to expressions of the brand. As in content experience design, look for a solid organizational structure to support the ongoing, consistently high-quality application of the brand, resulting in experiences that are even better because of it.

BRAND EXTENSION

Once the brand experience is **in market**, the organization may decide to use the same brand in a different market, with different products. Although the brand will continue to be known for the original product or service, it will be extended to a new or refreshed product line or category. A clear example was when Apple decided to start making phones under the Apple name. The reverse can also happen. For example, telecom providers have created a lower-end brand with simpler phone plans, but kept the original brand for the premium offering. This event would trigger the brand experience process to start again.

Chapter 6

THE ENGAGEMENT EXPERIENCE

In the experience thinking framework, we talk about four quadrants: brand, product, content, and service. All four cover a clear aspect of the experience. However, there is some room for another type of experience that floats between brand on the one hand, and product/content/service on the other. This is the engagement experience (plus related experiences such as onboarding, purchasing, and sales).

The engagement experience can be understood in two ways. First, we can think of engagement as being emotionally connected to a cause or an organization to the extent that the customer becomes a loyal advocate.

The second definition of "engagement" is similar to the one that occurs in the context of marriage. When two people get engaged, they are making a commitment and choosing to get married. Similarly, when a customer engages, they are choosing to experience the product, content, or service, and committing to the idea that the organization is worth their time and money.

Customers want to feel connected and be a part of something that makes their lives better. Branding is the first step toward connecting with a customer, but

Customers buy your product because they believe they want to be part of your ecosystem.

engagement is also important. Engagement creates the emotional attachments that lead to conversion. As the customer moves through the onboarding or sales funnel, the engagement experience helps them connect more and more with the organization until they have an undeniable desire to commit.

Engagement in a For-Profit Organization

The engagement experience in a for-profit organization is about how you bind the customer to your brand, product, or service, so you can ultimately make money as an organization. You want to determine the best ways to engage with your customer, communicate value, and create awareness around your brand/product in order to drive sales and loyalty.

Customers buy because they see value in your offering. This value can be calculated as the benefit they receive from your product divided by the money they must pay for it. When customers buy, you profit.

As you design for engagement, consider why the consumer wants to be a part of your organization. Try to discover why the customer would buy your product, and why they wouldn't. Ask them about the value they see in the product, and try to understand their attitudes and perceptions in the presales context. Use these insights to craft an experience that engages and builds connection.

The engagement experience addresses where value lies from the customer's perspective and the ways you might improve upon it.

Engagement in Government & Nonprofit Organizations

When an organization isn't profit-driven, their "business" is their mandate. For example, they may have a mandate to create awareness around certain topics, or a mandate to provide certain services to the public. They aren't selling a product. However, value is still an effective measure if it can be reframed as whether or not you are accomplishing your mission, or meeting your directive.

The inquiry when designing this type of experience is similar to the questions asked in the realm of for-profit organizations. Instead of customers, however, you want to understand the perceptions of citizens, members, or volunteers to determine if they are getting the best experience possible as they interact with you or receive your services. For the nonprofit organization or government agency, the questions become these: Are we meeting our mandate? Why does it matter? What is the citizen's perception of our purpose or vision? How are they helped? What is the strategy for accomplishing our mission?

Government agencies benefit from exploring and externalizing the real value they are creating. This means you need to get answers to your questions before jumping in to create solutions. Thinking and designing for the engagement experience helps you figure out why you are doing specific initiatives and how it will benefit your public.

Where Engagement Experiences Fit

The engagement experience is shared and overlaps in content, product, and service experiences. This is because each of those experiences will have an onboarding and/or buying phase that is part of the holistic lifecycle experience.

The engagement experience is such an important part of the overall experience that organizations will have people and departments devoted to its design and delivery. After all, where would the organization be if people didn't come through the door and start to engage with the brand, product, or service? Would it even exist? Probably not, so deep investments must be made into how to engage your audience.

Streamlining the experience of onboarding your customers with the experience of continued product use, support, and disposal/renewal/cancellation is where lifecycle experience design aligns the efforts and investments made by the organization.

Creating engagement ensures that your audience has a great experience from end-to-end.

The goal is to pull
them in and keep them
coming back for more.

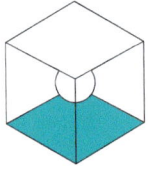

Chapter 7

EXPERIENCE THINKING FOR PRODUCT

Due to the complexity of technology and product design, it's difficult at the beginning of a project to predict the resulting experience for the user. However, if you engage users in the process as early as possible, you determine if the flow and interactions work as envisioned and deliver an intentional experience at launch.

Involve Users Early & Often

When a need for a new product arises, the first instinct is to start coming up with a design. However, the first design impulse is not necessarily the right solution, let alone the best solution. Exploration and deeper understanding is needed.

Finding out what a user wants, needs, or expects before creating the product is not a novel concept. Most organizations are on board with this idea, but they aren't used to involving the user *throughout* the development of the product. One belief is that users aren't experts and wouldn't be helpful after the initial discovery stages. Another is

User research focuses on ways to learn from the user at every point in the design process.

that involving users is a costly and time-consuming activity that slows down delivery.

Adherence to these ideas causes you to reduce or eliminate the involvement of users in the design and building phases of your product and not introduce them again until the beta testing stage or at launch. By then, there's a high risk of "getting it wrong." You thought you knew how the user would react to and interact with the experience without any evidence that this would be the case. You pushed the problem down the road but can't avoid it. At some point, your product or service will be used by customers and users, so why not stay in touch with them?

Staying connected to the behavior of users with your experience throughout the entire design process is the only way to know you're building the right thing. Without user insight and input, product designers will fall back on their own assumptions and opinions. If you keep users involved during design, however, you keep the conversations alive and will understand the complete picture that can provide specific answers.

When a plane takes off from New York to London, the path of the plane is not a direct line between the two end points. The plane must constantly make minor course corrections to adapt to any challenges on the journey. Similarly, involving users throughout will help you course-correct and recover from any mistakes in the understanding of user intention that you made in the beginning. You will save money because you are able to adjust as you go and arrive at the right destination.

You'll build and launch knowing that you are building and launching the right experience.

Even though you ask a user what they want in a product, the value statements they provide are usually too high-level to be directly useful. They'll say they want the product to be better, faster, or cheaper, but those terms are too vague to guide design. The critical question that you need to have answered through user involvement is how they will use the product.

More User Research

Users want ease of use. For the most part, companies know this and want the same thing. They will speak to their desire for products that are fast and efficient, but wishing doesn't make it so.

Once you define what constitutes ease of use, the question then becomes how to get there. The first step to fully understand and capture ease of use is to talk to potential users and find out how they think. What words or phrasing do they use? What is their mental model, or the way they explain how things work? There are several approaches that we can take to arrive at an understanding of user behavior.

Focus groups generally are not useful when trying to understand use. Instead, you want to learn from the user's continued use of the product, not just their first impressions. A product demonstration also isn't helpful, because the demonstrator always knows how the product works and ensures that the demonstration makes the product look as easy to use as possible.

Similarly, survey questionnaires aren't very effective. Users that answer surveys often skew their representations of the experience and end up saying the product is "pretty good." In the marketplace, "pretty good" isn't enough.

Define "ease of use" in a way that matches your user's expectations of how things should work, for them.

Observation is the key. The true picture only emerges when you actually watch the user as they use and experience the product or service. You'll be able to note exactly where the users stumble, and then design for those issues. The point of the observation is to reframe your data and raw technology in human terms.

Good user research often begins with in-depth, contextual interviews as well as ethnographic techniques, such as job shadowing, to understand a day in the life of a user and their interactions with the product. Starting with the wider questions of what user challenges exist, where things work, and where things break gives you that broader picture of where your product and service will fit. You get a sense of how the user will be helped by your solution, in their context of use.

Capture your understanding of the user and their behavior in user profiles (personas) and in usage scenarios. These initial insights will be instrumental in the creation of the preliminary design concepts. Once you have several design concepts, test the different usage scenarios with users. It's a process that is extremely effective as you start to create sketches, storyboards, and eventually a sequence of screens (wireframes), mock-ups, and prototypes that form the experience.

Applying a mix of business input *and* user input services the experience instead of the underlying technology. It's what smart companies do on a consistent basis. First, they find the value, and then they figure out the best experience that matches business, customer, and user requirements. Critical in all of this is keeping a direct line open with the customers and users as you go through the design and build phase, so you can get it right the first time you go to market.

PRODUCT

INNOVATION

Opportunity Discovery
Idea Scouting
Environment Immersion
Idea Capture

Idea Exploration
Experience Sketching
Experience Feasibility
Experience Roadmap

Concept Incubation
Concept Testing
Success Metrics
Business Case

BUILD

Experience Specification
Design Patterns
Design Style Guide
Design Specifications

Experience Support
UX Testing
Design Review
Detailed Design

RESEARCH
Ethnography
Interviews
Surveys
Contextual Inquiry
Focus Groups

TESTING
Prototype Testing
User Experience Testing

DESIGN

Interaction Design
Interaction Architecture
Navigation & Accessibility
Prototyping & Wireframing

Visual Design
Data Visualization
Visual Framework
Layouts & Elements

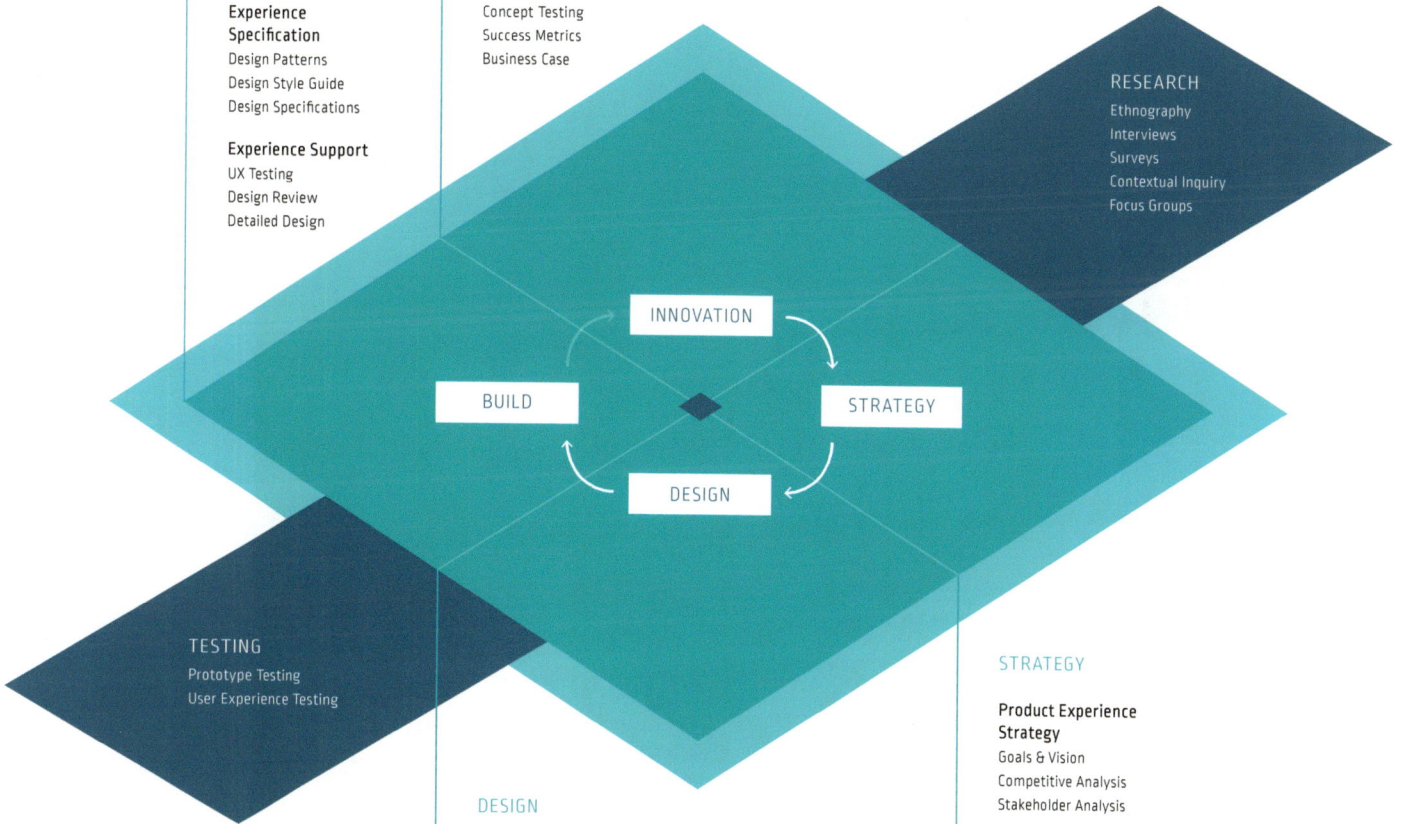

STRATEGY

Product Experience Strategy
Goals & Vision
Competitive Analysis
Stakeholder Analysis

Understanding Use
User Segments & Personas
User Tasks & Workflows
Product Experience Lifecycle
User Stories
Experience Journeys
User Requirements

INNOVATION
BUILD
STRATEGY
DESIGN

Experience Thinking Process

Product Experience in Eleven Steps

The product experience process has four main phases: innovation, strategy, design, and build. Product design is driven by innovations and in-market feedback to adjust, improve, and pivot the experience in order to stay relevant or become relevant. Product experiences typically follow brand experience design.

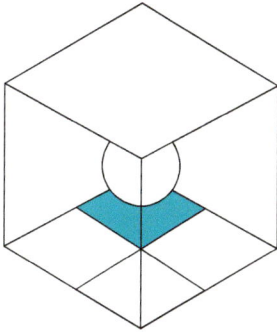

Innovation Phase

OPPORTUNITY DISCOVERY

The search, discovery, and identification of new opportunities for innovation is continuous. These opportunities can be **scouted** from unexpected places. They are regularly in plain sight and often come from customers and users being **immersed** in an experience. In product experiences, these innovations usually are technological and operational in nature, with a significant contribution from the business model side.

Where innovations come from is one thing, and what you do to turn them into viable experiences is quite another. Moving the initially unpolished innovation understanding through the creation process begins not only with their discovery, but also with a robust **capture** of innovative experience opportunities. If done well, the new experience will push boundaries, and as you look back to reflect, your assessment may identify probable future trends. Experience ideas help big thinking come to the surface. Most innovative experience ideas captured in this stage allow for further exploration. Innovative opportunities are just the beginning. While great as a start, they lack sufficient detail to be experienced in their current state.

IDEA EXPLORATION

This next step takes the opportunities and explores them at the experiential level.

Sketching, journey mapping, and storyboarding turn ideas into experiences at such a concrete level that business stakeholders and potential customers alike can review, reject, and iterate to ensure **feasibility**. Even at this early stage, these meaningful explorations will weed out the unachievable from the achievable experiences without committing much effort.

During this phase, depicting a dozen experience journeys is not unheard of. The experience journeys allow for good coverage of the lifecycle as both business and value-chain exploration ensure a strong connection to feasibility.

These results are put into an **experience roadmap** that becomes part of a future product strategy. The roadmap answers questions such as: Which experience would be attainable, and when? What future experiences are we actually talking about, and what lifecycle coverage would

this experience have for our audience? In short, the results map the opportunity space and fill it with experience ideas that start to have legs.

CONCEPT INCUBATION

In increasing amounts, business reality kicks in. Due to limited time and budget, there is a need to bring focus to early ideas and reduce the number of concepts that will be part of the **business case**. This happens through evaluation from an experience perspective.

Concept testing allows stakeholders to evaluate the strength of the experience. It takes place through participatory testing to ensure that customer and user reaction levels of input are on par with the business and technology factors.

Increasingly higher fidelity, but fewer, concepts create the best circumstance for the development of **success metrics**. Success metrics cover business, technology, *and* the experience goals. This produces a clear direction for further experience design in the following phases.

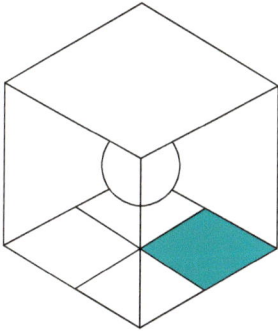

Strategy Phase

PRODUCT EXPERIENCE STRATEGY

With the early phases complete, you can start to look at defining a solution. The product strategy identifies and captures the **goals and vision** of the product experience. What is the intended experience? How does it impact the business, the audience, and the marketplace? Through **stakeholder analysis** you can capture key internal business requirements from all parts of the organization that have a stake in the delivered experience.

This will be accompanied by a **competitive analysis** of existing or similar offerings in the marketplace to complete the three key elements of a product strategy: goals and vision, internal business requirements, and outside market forces. All three elements are needed to form the strategy of what the product experience aspires to become.

UNDERSTANDING USE

The product experience revolves mostly around the user. Creating a desirable experience a user wants, with content and functions the user needs, always starts with understanding and capturing who your user really is. This user research results in the identification of **user segments and personas**. This is step one.

Step two goes beyond the *who* and into *what* the user specifically does to reach success on their terms. It also examines the *where*, or the environment (physical or otherwise).

This deep understanding of **users' tasks**, their **workflows**, and environment allows you to document the current state of the product experience from the point of view of the audience. You can then identify critical **user requirements** and consider better product opportunities in the experience design.

The last phase in strategy is preparing the analysis and user requirements for use in the design phase. The challenge is turning broad and deep insights into a direction for design.

First, create experience (or user) **stories** that describe specific usage situations. These are written at a level that allows you to design solutions, and they are key to prioritizing content and functionality in workflows and tasks with the product. Several of these user stories together form the basis of

the next level: **experience journeys** that a user goes through with the product.

And in turn, these journeys, linked with in-between experiences that connect them together, feed into the **experience lifecycle** map. In this phase, the lifecycle map captures the *use* of the product. This map will form the foundation of the overall experience that different audiences have with the product. The map will also include the engagement (or customer) experience phase. The combination of user experience and customer experience phases form the end-to-end experience lifecycle map of a product.

Understanding: Product Research

During both innovation and strategy phases we utilize several research techniques that involve the user. The focus of these research techniques is primarily on understanding what members of your audience *do*. How do they interact with information? How do they manipulate the information? How do they use the outcome to their benefit?

The nature of this type of research is typically observational combined with structured interviews that focus less on the attitude and perceptions of (potential) users and more on usability. To design products that show benefits and value to the *user*, you want to learn the most about the usability and usefulness of the experience to them.

User research is complementary to engagement/customer research, and both types should be considered in any product experience design initiative. Representative research techniques include task analysis, **interviews**, **ethnographic observation**, **contextual inquiry**, job shadowing, and apprenticeship approaches.

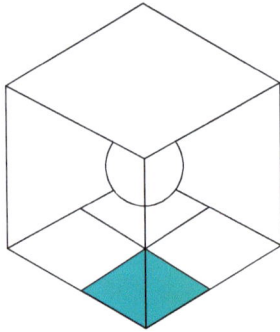

Design Phase

INTERACTION DESIGN

The transition from user requirements to initial designs is significant. Translating user stories and journeys into screens, physical artifacts, or space layouts requires the ability to deeply understand what insights were discovered and then turn these into creative shapes and forms that will deliver to those requirements. This doesn't happen immediately. It requires a degree of controlled trial and error to reach a sufficient experience quality.

We use this iterative process to design manipulation, successfully interacting with a screen, object, or function, and **navigation**, moving from one screen or step to the next. Successful design in these areas focuses on the target user groups of the experience so they can achieve their business-critical goals and workflows. The characteristics of the user groups will vary. For example, users may have differences in domain knowledge and cognitive ability, as well as physical ability, that may require consideration of **accessibility**.

These flows and interactions are designed with a specific concept in mind. **Interaction architecture** choices will influence the design: a combination of *process*-oriented design (wizard-like interactions with a strong flow order), *data*-oriented design (surfacing data and functions with limited structure), and *task*-oriented design (clustering content and functions according to the task at hand). Many designs aim to move away from data-oriented design toward process- and task-oriented design.

It is essential in iterative design to create, review, and re-create in a way that is lightweight and disposable. It allows for faster learning and achieves higher quality sooner. Therefore, create early **prototypes** and sketches or schematics of screens (**wireframes**) that do not have significant (or any) technology behind them. Instead, focus on the experience by the user. The wireframes capture the flow of interaction, what happens in sequence, and what steps the user must take to successfully complete their tasks and reach their goals.

VISUAL DESIGN

The second major phase in design is where task-based flows, labels, and content receive another layer of design that evokes emotion. Visual design adds a key ingredient to the design phase by creating and refining the visual elements (graphics, fonts, color palette, photography, typography, style guides, icons, etc.) and **data visualization** in general. It completes the product experience from a visceral and emotional perspective.

This is also a phase where the **layouts** and specific screen **elements** that shape the wireframes are reinterpreted and enhanced from a visual perspective. The experience becomes remarkable not only on a goal and task level, but also on an aesthetic level. A clear connection to the brand experience is made because the product experience is a manifestation of the brand experience and the brand promise.

The visual design phase can be the beginning of a system of product visuals. This **visual framework** is a library of visually connected elements that go beyond the singular product, but are present in service, content, and even engagement experiences of the organization.

Testing: Validating the Experience

Keeping the end user involved remains important during the design and the following construction phases. Each iterated design creates the risk of going off track, delivering less to the needs of the user. An ongoing feedback loop will keep everything aimed in the right direction.

A vital technique in this phase is **user experience testing** that involves users carrying out tasks in a controlled and observed interview setting. As you observe how they interact with the experience, you gain the feedback necessary to understand what works and what doesn't, and you can adjust the design accordingly.

Testing can be done with wireframes, **prototypes**, or final visuals in the design phase, and with coded experiences in the build phase, with more interactivity as the product is finalized. The test outcomes are fed back into the next iteration of the experience design. Improve your experiences and repeat this approach for as long as the project constraints allow.

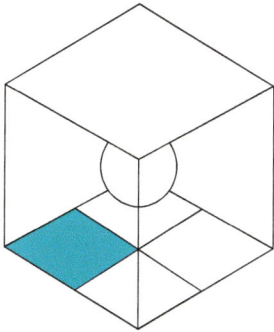

Build Phase

EXPERIENCE SPECIFICATION

Based on the final visual designs, the coding phases in terms of experience design primarily focus on the presentation or front-end code. **Design specifications** are a combination of annotated wireframes that show clearly how the flow of content and functions work from a user's perspective, and a limited set of coded visual pages or **designed patterns** that capture the visual framework of the product experience. These patterns capture reusable components for the product experience (e.g., search, selection, navigation, e-commerce design patterns). Depending on the collaborative nature of the coding team, there may be more or fewer detailed specifications needed to support the build phase.

A **design style guide** is a good deliverable to make the experience design less dependent on the team that originally created it. It can be used to more formally capture the visual framework and specific data visualizations used in the design. The goal is to keep the design intent intact from the design phase to product launch. Experience design quality is all about minding the details. Having a brilliant design slightly reinterpreted in code reduces the quality in most cases.

EXPERIENCE SUPPORT

Throughout construction, coding, engineering, and manufacturing, you will support and monitor the quality of development of the experience. This is done with ongoing **detailed design** support, where the designers will provide additional elements (like icons, customized design patterns, partial page layout design) where needed.

In both waterfall and agile environments, the designers will do frequent check-in or **design reviews** to keep the design at the intended quality level and to support the code testing team.

Finally, the **user experience testing** happens at least once during the build phase. The product performance from a code perspective will influence the experience, so it is critical to test with users in this phase. Testing at this point will make sure any design adjustment can still be made before the product goes to market.

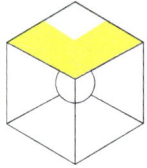

Chapter 8

EXPERIENCE THINKING FOR CONTENT

If you've ever been on a website and couldn't find an answer, or could find only outdated and irrelevant information, you've experienced a content problem. Content is the information managed, changed, sorted, and delivered by your website, app, service, or product. This information includes text, images, video, audio, and other media.

The aim is to *design* your content so it enhances the product and service experience. Another aim is to *structure* the content so it enhances the experience. At times, the content *is* the experience to a large extent, like in news websites, or movie and TV show websites. In others, it's a part of the experience, like in online banking or when paying a parking ticket online.

In any of these cases, you can't create a service or product experience without distinctly designing for content. Content requires its own design process that is intertwined with the product design and service design efforts.

Information Architecture

A key aspect of content is the information architecture. This is the way you structure information as well as the words and labels you use to describe the information. Information is often structured in a hierarchical way. This seems rather navigational because users will be scrolling around and drilling into lower levels looking for information. Before this navigation, however, you want to know and capture how the information chunks relate to each other, and if the information is structured in a way that is easy to find and combine. The actual user action of navigating through and manipulating the information is part of interaction design and is addressed in the *product experience* quadrant.

Users want to be able to browse in a way that makes sense to them. Again, you have to understand how people think so you can match the way they will try to find your information. The terminologies people use over and over are the ones you need to know. Start by researching hierarchies of words that people use and understand, and then test them with users before you start to design the product or service.

There are technical and formal terms for things, and there are ways people actually speak when they describe an item. For example, you might need one of those things that goes on the end of the garden hose to spray water. Although your store sells these *nozzles*, your customer doesn't know that is the name for the product. So how can you make it easy for your customer to navigate your website and find all of the great nozzles you have for sale? You have to speak their language.

The nonprofit sector is no different. If you have a municipal website, your constituents will not be well served if they are searching for "trash," and the information they need is under "garbage disposal."

Your research and observations help you understand how your audience requests and interacts with information. You can use this research to group and structure your information more meaningfully. This quadrant is not concerned with finding the answer at the navigational level. Instead, the question right now is whether the right content is on the screen regardless of what it looks like and how the user got there. Later, we will design for navigation and presentation of the information.

Match User Expectations

The amount of content that organizations handle can be staggering. For example, Amazon must be very strategic regarding the management of its information, or the site will quickly become outdated and irrelevant.

Netflix is in a similar position. Although the site needs to look good, it's more important that the content is appropriate and viewers can easily find the movie that's right for them. Netflix is content-heavy, so it has to strategically group movies and television shows in a way that makes sense to their users, or the users will be overwhelmed. The way they build trust with their audience is by grouping their programs in ways that match the grouping that the users expect.

There's another specific research technique useful in this area called *card sorting*, in which you have users group labels or words. For example, Netflix might have their test group of users sort films and television shows according to category, such as whether the show fits into groupings of drama, comedy, crime, or science fiction.

Content research and design is not only useful in the digital space; it's also applicable to products. When you go to the grocery store to pick up something to make a sandwich, don't you expect to find the peanut butter next to the jelly? This is a content decision that the store has made. Although it might

It's not difficult to find out what your users' expectations are, or how they want to access your content. You ask them, and you watch them use your content.

logically make sense for the peanut butter to be near the peanuts, or the grape jelly to be with the grapes, the shopper expects something different. The most successful stores reflect the mindset of their customers.

Content Management & Governance

To mature as an organization in content handling, you have to make conscious decisions regarding the management and governance of your content if you want your site to stay relevant and valuable.

The first part of content governance is making decisions about retention and archiving content. What will you save, and how will that decision be made? How will you assess your content and replace outdated content? What rules can you put in place to prevent redundancy of materials and to avoid becoming a digital archive? Websites grow unmanageable very quickly without checks in place to oversee the ever-growing content.

The second part of governance is about the creation of content. Instead of making ad hoc decisions about whether additional content can be shared and where it will reside, create a process of review. Make it very clear in your organization who owns the information so the right people are in place for sign-off and approval.

Above are key elements for designing and managing your content. There is a growing recognition that content is distinct from product and service and needs its own strategy, research, and design process. The content process described in the next section, along with the product and service design processes, will complete the design for your end-to-end experience lifecycle.

CONTENT

Content Migration
Moving Content
QA & Testing
Content Compliance

Content Management
Experience Optimization
Governance Communication
Retention Policies
On-the-job Support
Training

RESEARCH
Web Analytics
Interviews
Workshops
Card Sorting

MANAGEMENT

STRATEGY

DESIGN

TESTING
Pilot Projects
Role Playing
Simulation Workshops
Reverse Card Sorting
UX Testing

DESIGN

Content Architecture
Detailed Structure
Tone, Voice & Positioning

Content Design
Content Review (ROT)
Content Mapping
Content Vetting

Content Creation
Net-new
Rewrite
Content Style Guide

STRATEGY

Content Strategy
Vision Articulation
Stakeholder Analysis
Competitive Landscape

Governance Framework
As-is Processes
To-be Processes
Workflows

Content Planning
Content Audit
Content Migration Plan
System Customization

Experience Thinking Process

Content Experience in Ten Steps

The content experience process has three main phases: strategy, design, and management. There's no up-front innovation phase because content follows a "create-review-revise" pattern as opposed to the concept of the "what if we do this" experience as a whole. Content experiences typically follow product and service experience creation.

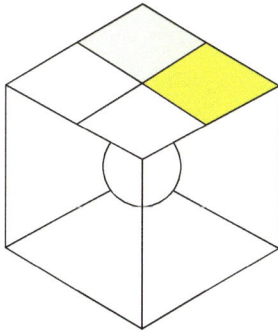

Strategy Phase

CONTENT STRATEGY

In this phase, you will capture a specific strategy for all content in the experience. Content follows both the product and service **vision and mission**, but it has its own goals and direction. From a content perspective, what voice, tone, and positioning do you want? How does the content enhance the experience? What is the content direction in these major types of media: text, image, animation, photo, and video?

To answer these questions, gather input from internal and external **stakeholder analysis** interviews and workshops, and assess the **competitive landscape** from a content perspective. How are similar organizations or entities we aim to emulate working with their content? What can we learn from them? The content strategy feeds these insights in order to capture the core content goals and the vision of what the overall content experience will be.

GOVERNANCE FRAMEWORK

Part of a strategy phase specific to content is governance. In this context, governance is a set of processes and steps that guides the creation, vetting, and publishing of any content in the experience. These processes need to be designed early in content experience projects and refined throughout. Governance will form the framework to keep content relevant and current not only at launch, but also at any future experience point. The importance of content in experiences is ever growing, so it demands its own process.

The first step in creating a governance framework is understanding the current **as-is process** of content creation in the organization. Who is currently involved in creation? How are decisions made around content publishing? How do we ensure today that new and revised content fits well with the overall experience? This activity of interviews, surveys, and workshops usually results in a spotty picture of the organization, ranging from highly organized and mature content creation, to chaotic or ad hoc content creation and management.

The second step in the governance framework is capturing the **to-be processes** for content. At the future launch of this experience,

how will you need or want to manage your content creation, vetting, and publishing? The future *to-be* governance framework at this point is in the shape of a plan, or a strategy. Don't execute on this plan until you are in the design and management phases, but start defining the framework now to be ready to pilot and further roll out the framework during these later phases.

Both the *as-is* and *to-be* process analyses need to be detailed. The **workflows** that you capture (formal and informal) from stakeholders need a level of granularity, not often found in other design processes. This stems from the multistakeholder, multiprovider nature of content creation. Content that ultimately ends up on a single platform can come from dozens of sources and teams, each going through its own creation, vetting, and publishing process.

Mapping out the processes is a daunting task. It requires a structured approach in order to capture essential elements of governance across the board, as well as to compare and capture all of the stakeholder teams needed. You also need to associate responsibilities to deliverables. This mapping can greatly assist you in creating a cohesive picture of the roles and responsibilities on the team, how the team communicates and comes to decisions, and how to adjust for *to-be* processes. Answering these questions will set up the organization for effective content management and governance in the future.

CONTENT PLANNING

Without diving in to create or update content, this strategic phase is about bringing focus to assess your content and plan concretely for the design phase. Broad strokes are used in determining how the overall content will be managed from current to future states. Content curation, migration planning, and system customization are brought into the project scope and plan.

The first activity is conducting a **content audit** to review current content from a relevancy perspective. How can you make the current body of content as relevant as possible? Assessing the importance, relevance, and popularity of all content in the experience will help you understand where to enhance, reposition, or remove content. This can mean a rewrite of content, but also a repackaging of content from text to animation, graphs, or video, and vice versa. The audit uses findings from call center logs, web traffic analytics, search analytics, customer service interactions, social media ratings, and user recommendations.

The content audit cannot stand on its own. A **content migration plan** must be created to determine the size and scope of any content updates. The plan will answer the following questions: What are the consequences of the content audit? What does it mean in terms of effort and time if we enhance, reposition, or remove all content identified in the audit? Which areas need more attention, and which are good enough? The content migration plan keeps you grounded so you don't get stalled in trying to meet unattainable goals.

The result is an attainable plan to deliver the best content experience within project boundaries.

The migration plan also has a direct impact on the technical system that holds your content, regardless of whether it is paper-based, digital-based, enterprise-level, user-generated, text, photos, graphics, or videos. The implications for those systems become much clearer with the availability of the migration plan. This step assesses and plans for **customizations** to internal content **systems**, materials, and areas that are impacted by the content strategy including training, change management, and knowledge management.

Understanding: Content Research

The strategy phase needs input from business stakeholders and staff as well as data from various content sources. This content research includes insights learned from **web analytics**, search analytics, stakeholder **interviews**, and **workshops**. The analytics are typically captured in online tools and continually monitored to understand how users navigate through the content, where they click, and what search terms they use to reach pertinent content, as well as to show the high-level connection between audience demographics and where they navigate.

The first set of research techniques is complemented with a specific, narrower research technique called card sorting.

This research supports the information or content architecture step in the design phase. In **card sorting** research, the user is asked to *group* content together in a way that makes sense to them. These groups can then be given a title by the user to provide further insight into how the user sees the content structure. The resulting structure captures where content needs to go together, where it doesn't, and how strong the bond is between groups of content. This research tool jump-starts the next phase: design.

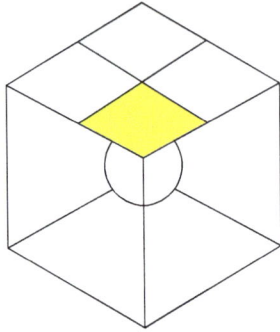

Design Phase

CONTENT ARCHITECTURE

When the final card sorting research is complete, you can create a **detailed content structure**. The structure of content is written to match the knowledge and language skills of the intended end user. It supports users' information needs and provides content where users expect to find it.

At this point, it's not important how a specific page layout supports the user or how the user navigates between pieces of content. Focus instead on the hierarchy and structure of the content blocks, where types of content would be housed, and how close or far apart they sit in the overall content structure. It's truly the architecture of the content and the blueprint of a map showing where to find it.

This content architecture step is also an excellent time to start thinking about the overall character of the content. What is the **tone of voice**? Is it **positioned** as content that is formal, casual, technical, and/or concise? The tone influences the content labels, menus, and headings, which in turn impact the content structure and how or where users will find relevant content for them. It's all connected. Using "factually correct" labels that have a high degree of jargon built in creates a risk that content will not be discovered, or that it will be wrongly judged as being the right information. This issue can create unintended and serious consequences, particularly in the areas of taxes or health information.

The resulting structure forms the content architecture that is the basis for the next step: content design. At this point, content architecture needs to be checked against the content strategy, so both stay aligned going forward.

CONTENT DESIGN

The content architecture provides the bones, but the content design step provides a more detailed view on how the content is structured at the document, section, and page level. Content design makes sure that your content is meeting the needs of your audience.

In this activity, the **content** is **reviewed** page by page, section by section, document by document for redundant, outdated, or trivial content (**ROT**). Any content that is no longer required is removed or updated. Using the governance framework as created in the strategy phase, you will involve the right content owners and stakeholders to make the decision of updating or removing content.

In conjunction with the content review, the team now **maps** all **content** that needs to move from its old location in the current architecture to the new architecture location based on the redesigned content architecture. This content mapping is comprehensive and sometimes extensive in the case of an intranet or large corporate website. It usually requires large spreadsheets and many work hours to capture all of the content. You will also make the determination whether any content is feasibly better delivered through graphics, animations, or video.

The final activity in this step is making sure that the content is accurate, fit for purpose, and complete, and that you have buy-in from the organization. **Content vetting** happens by business, legal, human resources, compliance, health, safety, finance, and numerous other subject-matter stakeholders in the organization. The goal is both to deliver the highest possible quality of content to the audience and to reduce any harmful exposure to the organization from the outside world. The vetted content is then housed in many documents and content management system containers for future use. The combination of content reviews, mapping, and vetting results in a solid foundation of content that will be augmented with the results of the next step: content creation.

CONTENT CREATION

The earlier step of content design focused on existing content, but content creation utilizes the previously identified content gaps to write **net-new** content to address the holes. The writing is usually done by the content owners, the teams that know it best and can write for their audience, but hired copywriters or specialized technical writers may supplement the team. All content writers work on specific content creation, making sure it is optimized for different devices (like mobile). They may also work on potential translations and potentially work with graphic designers and video creators to deliver content in the best formats for the audience.

Many times, there is no need for a completely new writing of content. Instead, a **rewrite** of existing content may be all that is needed to update or augment the information to be useful in the current environment. This is usually a bigger part of the content creation step and one that requires repeated reviews since formerly approved content is being changed. Governance is particularly important at this point. The more deliberately the process is managed, the more likely you are to remain on schedule.

Both rewrites and net-new content are greatly helped by a consistent tone, style, and approach. A **content style guide** can capture the tone and writing style of the organization and aid in the training of writers and reviewers alike. The style guide also helps in building a shared culture regarding the writing approach for different media and purposes. In most organizations, subject-matter experts write the published material because there are no trained writers on staff. The guide presents an expression of the content strategy and aims to align the writing styles of different departments.

Testing: QA for Content

This phase is about considering the content as part of the overall experience, and then testing the quality of the content as it sits within that experience. This is done through **user experience testing** where the user is asked to conduct tasks with the content. Here we learn if the content does its job. Is it legible? Is it applicable? Does it create user experience challenges that impede a good experience?

A **reverse card sort** or tree testing is a narrower testing tool used to confirm that content architecture performs as required. In this test, we remove the page layout and only show the user a bare-bones hierarchy of labels. The user tests the comprehension of these labels as they navigate the content hierarchy. For example, will the user be able to find the tomato under "fruits," or under "vegetables"?

You can also test the organizational environment for managing published content. What would day-to-day management of content actually look like? One approach is to conduct **role playing** and a **simulation workshop** to literally walk through the process of updating, vetting, reviewing, and publishing content. This involves people, systems, and the content itself. How long does it take? Who is involved in following our governance framework? How do we address last-minute requests or crisis situations?

A second approach is to run longitudinal **pilot projects** to monitor over several days, weeks, or months to see how content management performs in real business circumstances. These pilots can be replicated in several departments and with different audiences to work out any governance issues, improve content retention policies, and improve processes.

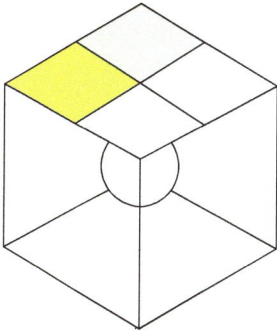

Management Phase

CONTENT MIGRATION

After the design phase, the management of your content is addressed. The first step in content migration is to make sure the newly written and/or rewritten content ends up in the right spot in the content architecture. The activity of **moving content** can take a few months or more than a year, depending on the amount of content being moved and how the net-new content is intertwined with existing content.

The moved content needs several rounds of **QA and testing**, for basic aspects such as spelling and grammar, as well as for consistent nomenclature, style, user experience, and structure throughout the content. This testing is a combination of automated tools and human reviewers. As edits are made, business stakeholders and subject-matter experts are called upon to sign off on the changes once again.

Finally, a specific type of testing for **compliance** is used to scan the content for certain phrases, statements, or information that might be harmful to the organization due to confidentiality or privacy concerns. Compliancy tests are part of the governance framework and would need further refinement and continuous monitoring as future content is added and edited.

CONTENT MANAGEMENT

Once the new content is up, it is continuously monitored and **optimized** based on site and search analytics, iterative experience testing, and other continuous improvement mechanisms. This is an ongoing activity throughout the lifecycle of the content.

In this phase, you are trying to solidify the ongoing execution of your governance framework. **Governance communication** and **training** become important as you complete a change management program to have the organization manage content effectively and efficiently. The stakeholders immediately integrate content management practices, as well as provide future

on-the-job support to keep the skill level high throughout the organization.

The last step in the content experience process is setting up the **content retention policies**. Once you determine how long the content stays active, you will have complete management of the entire content lifecycle.

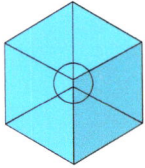

Chapter 9

EXPERIENCE THINKING FOR SERVICE

The service experience quadrant puts content and product experiences in a holistic end-to-end context. A service can contain multiple product experiences and multiple content experiences, as well as other intangible or non-product experiences.

All of these make up the service experience. For example, think of customer service and how it applies in a restaurant or hotel experience. These organizations can have concrete products like spaces, information boards, and websites, but the service experience also includes how the staff approaches you, how friendly they are, and how they try to make your experience as pleasant as possible.

Customers buy and users interact, but advocates connect with the service experience and become loyal.

The service experience quadrant is another lens to observe what the audience goes through. It's not only about individual products and specific content, or how to make money and create value. It's about designing all of those experiences *and* the glue that ties those experiences together to make them work successfully in a connected, holistic experience. This is why organizations increasingly look at

Many service experience journeys have the overarching goal of turning initial customers and users into long-term advocates of your organization.

designing for a service to better align often-separate and possibly disjointed experiences.

When we talk about service in the context of experience design, the conversation is about the customer's journey. The steps the customer takes must be intentionally linked in a coherent way. Your design needs to connect the points of the experience in a way such that the customer has no confusion about where to go or what to do next.

Example of a Service Experience

Service can be a nebulous concept because you don't really know what it is until you've experienced it.

For example, going to a restaurant includes various products—all designed at the product level—that together form the service experience. When you walk into a restaurant, you are met by the host who welcomes you to the restaurant. He then acts as the connector that takes you to your table. The table and chairs are a product experience in themselves, which you experience as you sit down.

LIFECYCLE

JOURNEYS

● Product Experiences

● Experience Connectors

EXPERIENCE OF A RESTAURANT VISIT

TRIGGER > **RESEARCH** > **TRAVEL** > **ENTER** > **ORDER** > **ENJOY** > **PAY** > **TRAVEL** > **REVIEW**

Planning to eat	Dining at the restaurant	Reflecting on experience

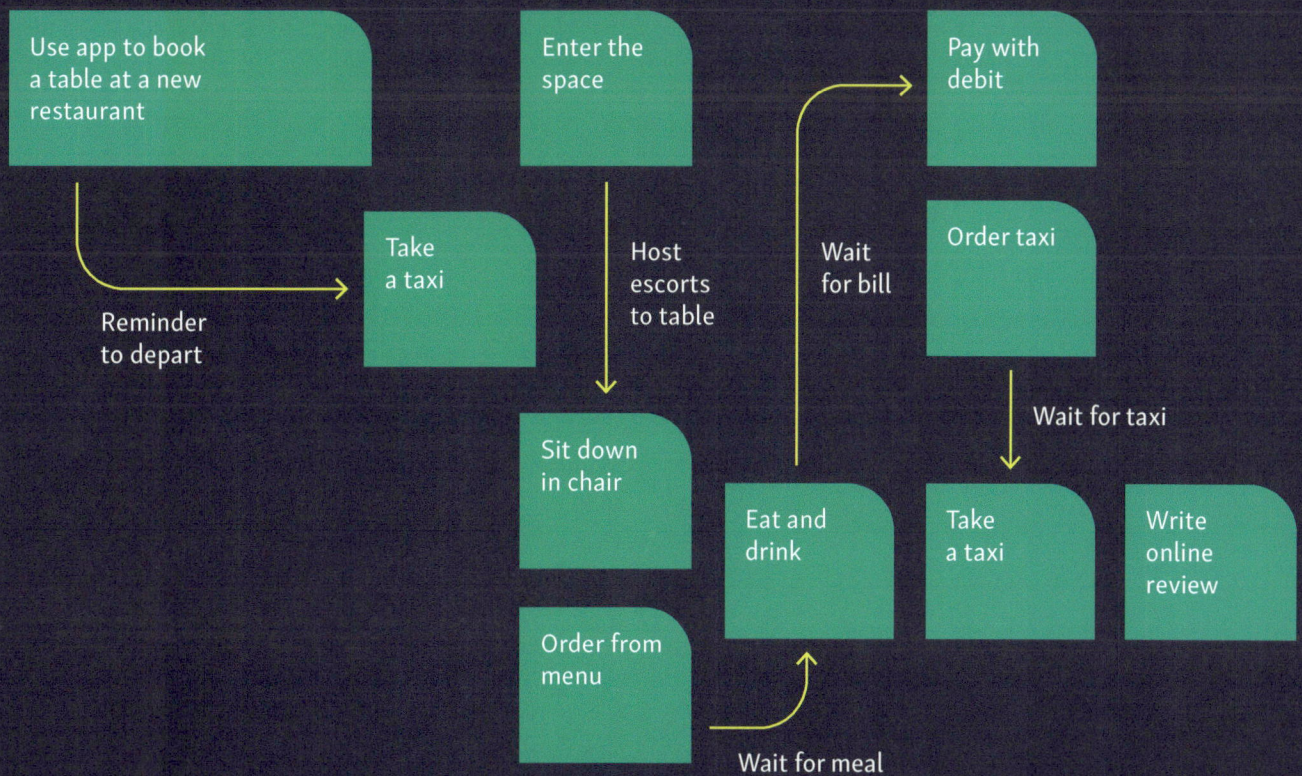

Use app to book a table at a new restaurant

Reminder to depart

Take a taxi

Enter the space

Host escorts to table

Sit down in chair

Order from menu

Wait for meal

Eat and drink

Wait for bill

Pay with debit

Order taxi

Wait for taxi

Take a taxi

Write online review

The waiter will make you comfortable, offer a glass of water, and give you a menu. The menu design is a product experience. The waiter takes your order, and after some time, brings it to your table for you to have the food experience. After some refills, ordering the dessert, and then perhaps ordering coffee or something stronger, you wave the waiter over once again to finally make your payment. The payment machine is also a product experience.

In the course of one meal, you had experiences with many different types of products. By designing for the service experience, the restaurant has a way of making sure nothing is missed. A successful restaurant is more than just good food. The furniture must be comfortable, the waiter must be helpful, the menu must be readable, and the checkout must be efficient. All of these things are connected and result in an overall perception of the restaurant and the service experience it offers.

The Big Picture

The service experience is the "big picture" that links all of the interactions that a person has with your organization. Because customers experience your organization in a linear way as they move from one point to the next, you should design and evaluate the service experience as one holistic experience.

Think of your users' journey as a red thread with each point of interaction as a knot. The service experience represents the red thread. You can't just define the points, however. The idea of the red thread is also to define the connectors that enable flow between the points.

If you are dealing with end-to-end experiences, you have to connect the points. Recognize that the red thread exists and is ultimately how your brand evolves—it's the culmination of your audience's perceptions,

experiences, and attitudes created by the service they receive. Organizations that keep departments in individual silos, working and designing solutions in isolation, miss the best opportunity to reach their audience and affect their brand in a positive way.

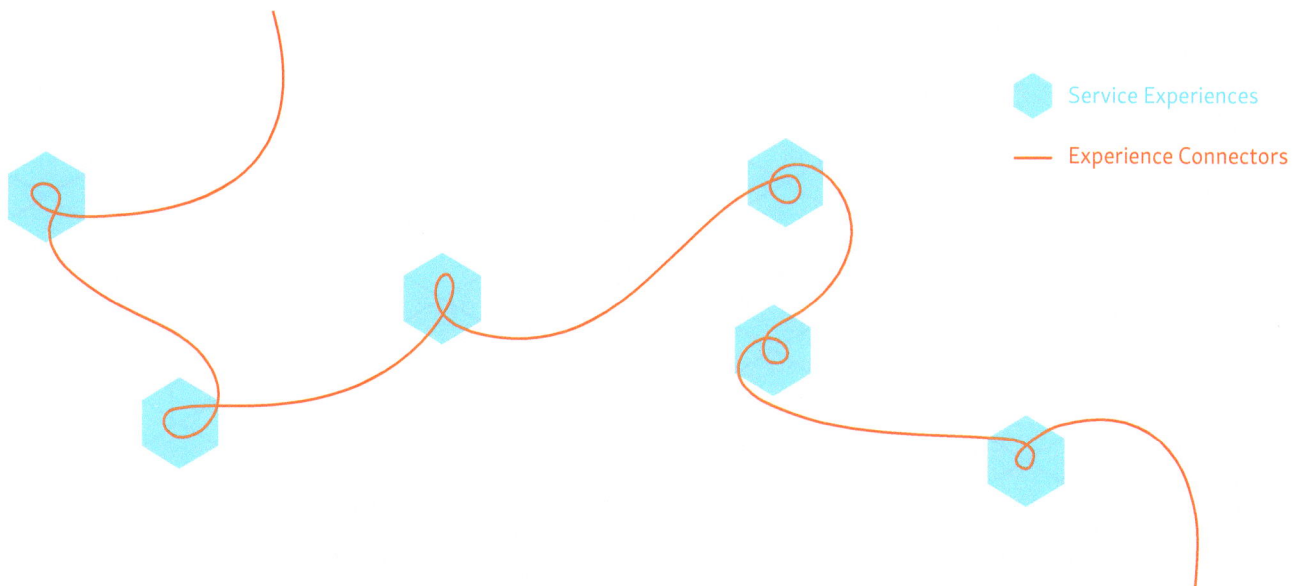

Service Experiences

Experience Connectors

If you thoroughly design for the service experience, you can make sure all of your products are working together to keep your customers coming back for more. Although departments may be responsible for individual products, they usually don't have an overarching mandate for the whole. Something will inevitably be lost in translation unless you use the service experience as a view to provide a high-level perspective. Increased connectivity will make all of your products and content operate as one cohesive service experience.

SERVICE

INNOVATION

Service Discovery
Envisioning Opportunities
Environment Disruption
Trend & Intelligence Scan

Exploration & Selection
Experience Options
Stakeholder Buy-in
Key Success Metrics

RESEARCH
Workshops & Interviews
Experience Mapping
Contextual Inquiry
Mystery Shopping
Ethnography
Focus Groups
Surveys

DELIVERY

Experience Specification
Service Patterns
Service Specifications
Service Experience Guidelines

Delivery Support
QA & Review
Design Support
Experience Testing

INNOVATION

DELIVERY

STRATEGY

DESIGN

STRATEGY

Service Experience Strategy
Goals & Vision
Stakeholder Analysis
Competitive Landscape

Understanding Journeys
Service Journeys
Service Lifecycle
Customer & User Personas
Customer & User Scenarios

TESTING
Service Role Playing
Service Staging
Service Walkthrough

DESIGN

Service Architecture
Service Lifecycle
Service Blueprint
Service Structure

Journey Design
Brand Experiences
Experience Connections
Product Experiences
Content Experiences

Experience Thinking Process

Service Experience in Ten Steps

The service experience process has four main phases: innovation, strategy, design, and delivery. You can think of service experience design as the big picture view of the experience you offer. Service design typically contains one or more product and content experiences.

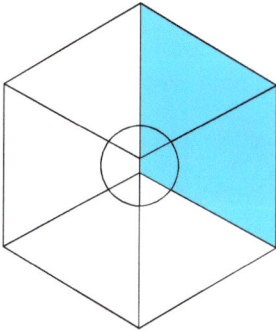

Innovation Phase

SERVICE DISCOVERY

Just as for product and content, we continuously search for new opportunities for innovation. In service experiences, the opportunities present themselves through new products and content, but also through business and market changes. The main difference between product and content innovations and service innovations is that in service experiences, the innovation can be lying further below the surface. It's not always as obvious where the innovation really is at

first glance. The whole can turn out to be of much greater impact than the parts alone.

In service discovery, the reason to create a new service experience can be driven by several factors. The first one is an outside **disruption in the environment**, such as something another organization does, an event that happens in society or the marketplace, or a legislative change in government policies. Any of these can cause a rethink of the status quo and create the need for action to engage your audience differently with an updated and improved service experience.

Similarly, the impetus to start a service experience initiative can come from a concerted effort driven from within the organization. Through research via either an ad hoc or a regular **scan of market intelligence and trends**, you reach the conclusion that there is a (renewed) need to engage your audience and consider a service design initiative. In optimal circumstances this could lead to proactive initiatives that help organizations take a lead in their sector.

A third motivation to begin creating a new service experience typically comes from stakeholders in a leadership role in an organization. The new initiative is an answer to their drive to innovate and lead through one or more best-in-class experiences with your audience. Here, the ambition comes from **envisioning** future **opportunities** for a service experience that is distinctive and remarkable and will set you apart from others. In these cases, the decision to act is based on an emerging vision for the organization.

EXPLORATION & SELECTION

Out of the experience discovery step, there may be enough reason to continue to explore the experience potential. If so, you will

engage relevant stakeholders to determine the types of experience that would have high potential to meet organizational goals.

The first activity is an exploration of distinct **experience options** with stakeholders. Conducting collaborative sessions in a creative workshop format will capture the anticipated experiences. The results will then be narrowed to a short list of reasonable approaches for consideration. The key element here is conceiving what the experience will look and feel like, without really building it. Other elements such as channel choices, audience reach, and service experience duration are also covered with the goal of a best-fit approach given time, budget, and anticipated scope.

The short-listed options are captured and provide input for the necessary **stakeholder buy-in** to move forward to selecting the most suitable experience to meet business goals. The purpose of the innovation phase is to make the experience concrete enough so that stakeholders can make informed decisions regarding whether an initiative can move forward to execution.

The buy-in of the stakeholder is partly driven by the understanding and expression of the **key success metrics**. What will success look like for the stakeholder group? How will we know that we are "there"? These metrics usually evolve during the project, but having an up-front and foundational understanding on how we measure success is critical to the overall actual and perceived impact of this initiative.

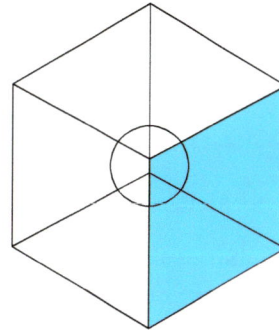

Strategy Phase

SERVICE EXPERIENCE STRATEGY

After we select a suitable experience in the innovation phase, the strategy phase includes the initial steps of planning and research for execution. The service experience strategy articulates the concrete **goals and vision** for the experience. What are the purpose and goals of the experience in the business context and the audience context?

Through **stakeholder analysis** you discover how internal and external stakeholders perceive the impact of the new service experience on the organization, the target audience, and teams in general. Key internal business requirements are also captured from all parts in the organization.

The last deliverable that is part of the service experience strategy is a **competitive landscape** of experiences from other organizations. This allows you to later assess the experience compared to these similar experiences, although the similarity may only be in some aspects. Together they capture what the experience aspires to be for the intended audiences, both internal for employees and external to the organization.

UNDERSTANDING JOURNEYS

Once the high-level direction is set, the attention shifts toward understanding what the real user and customer needs are for your service. What information do they look for?

What transaction or interactions are needed? Which groups of users are looking more for this type of service than others? Which customer groups may be more engaged to experience the service? The research with users and customers will identify your set of distinct **customer and user personas**, which are used as a guide to understand, in detail, how each group connects with your service.

Understanding the interactions will help you build the experience flow from beginning to end, and the result is a full-blown understanding of the end-to-end **service experience lifecycle** phases for the service. The experience lifecycle map captures all of the phases, emotions, and interactions (or experience points) that a customer and user go through before, during, and after using the service. This creates a robust framework to position each more-detailed experience element (i.e., journeys, scenarios, experience connectors, experience points) that makes up the overall lifecycle. In addition to the service experience, this map also includes product and content experience phases and activities where applicable.

The last phase in this strategy reaches such a level of granularity of understanding of the intended service experience that you can provide direct guidance and requirements to be used in the design phase. Each research insight feeds into detailed **customer and user scenarios** that capture what customers and users would do during their interactions with the organization. You will then be able to form a firmer understanding of what specific experiences are needed to reach their goals.

This set of scenarios also captures the experience journeys that a customer and user go through with a service or engagement. The journeys are one level down from a lifecycle as they capture a specific set

of scenarios and activities centered around a specific goal (i.e., the "pay-a-bill journey" as part of the bigger "driver's license renewal lifecycle"). These **service journeys** are linked together by connecting experiences to create a continuous and holistic experience for our audiences.

Understanding: Service Research

The first two phases are supported by various research techniques. These research techniques involve the business stakeholder, the end user, and the customer in order to de-risk the outcomes as much as possible.

In contrast to product experience design, in service experience design the focus of the research techniques is primarily on not only understanding what members of your audience do and how they interact with products and content, but also how they move between the products and content that make up the service experience. This is the key difference between services and products/content. The service research tries to understand the bridge between several products and pieces of content and their connectedness in the service experience.

The nature of this type of research is observational, asking, and participatory and includes **ethnographic approaches**, **interviews**, **focus groups**, and internal and external stakeholders' collaborations to understand requirements, business context, and experiences together. They result in an **experience map** of the holistic lifecycle and form the basis to be further validated, with additional interviews and observations, and quantified, through **surveys** with customers and users. These techniques provide a mix of attitude, perception, and behavior research.

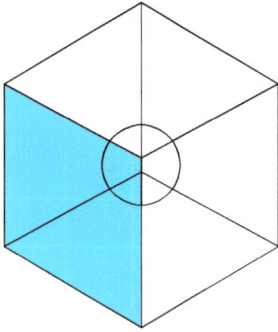

Design Phase

SERVICE ARCHITECTURE

The transition from understanding the service journeys to initial designs is considerable. Once you have captured customer and user personas, the service experience lifecycle, and an inventory of service experience journeys and scenarios, you can create the delivery side of the experience.

The first step of this phase is creating the foundational architecture for the service. Similar to capturing the experience lifecycle and journeys through experience mapping,

the focus here is on how we enable or deliver the service experience from an organizational perspective, as opposed to the external "experience" part of the service offering. This is captured in a **service blueprint**.

The blueprint captures how the experience will be delivered, from the organizational structure (people, business models, operational processes, enabling technology, and content) to how the different experiences concretely come to life for our audiences. The blueprint captures what we need to do as an organization to make this service experience a reality, and to keep it awesome for years to come.

The foundation is designed from the ground up as we create the blueprint, but a **service structure** is necessary to be successful. In creating a sustainable structure for the service, the initial challenge is the articulation of the **business** component. What is the organization trying to achieve with this service? What mandate is the service helping to reach? What business goal will be served with this experience?

The structure also has a **people** component. In this component, you estimate how much staff is required in specific job roles to support the service. What skill sets are needed? What level of experience, training, and knowledge is required?

There's also a **technology** component in this mix, which is potentially quite large. The questions to be addressed include these: What kind of technology is required for specific service elements? How is the technology connected to other systems? How are we developing and maintaining the technology needed?

With people and technology comes process. The **process** component covers each task, procedure, and workflow that needs to be designed from scratch in new service experiences, or redesigned and adapted in existing flows. You must determine what is new, what stays, and what changes.

The second component of the blueprint is the **service lifecycle**, and it's based on the version created during the strategy phase. While in the strategy phase, we focused on the experience for the customer and user. In the design phase, however, we map the internal structure to the external experience that customers and users go through. The goal is to make sure that the structure really can support the experience, and the focus is on designing the underlying structure as well as the resulting experience lifecycle.

Together, these components form the service architecture, the foundational structure that allows us to design for specific journeys in the next step in this phase.

JOURNEY DESIGN

The second step in the design phase moves the architecture (including the blueprint) forward to plan and design a program of experiences: product, content, brand, and connections. For each journey, the specific experiences are designed so that a planned combination of **product experience**, **content experience**, **brand experience**, and **connecting experiences** deliver to each element in the blueprint design. These journeys can be in sequence, overlap, stand alone, or have a connecting experience at the beginning or end that is specifically designed to make the transition from one customer or user journey to the next as effortless as possible.

For each product and content experience, you will design prototypes and mock-ups that allow for testing with customers and users. These holistic service experience designs undergo iteration and improvements until they are ready for the next phase: delivery.

Testing: Validating the Experience

Throughout design and, later, delivery, the aim is keeping the end user and customer involved. With each design iteration, it's helpful to touch base with the customer and user to make sure you stay on course and deliver to their goals and not the goals you assume or invent along the way. Service testing techniques ensure that you stay on track in numerous ways.

Earlier testing techniques of service design are conceptual in nature and focus on exploring and testing possible service scenarios and journeys beyond what was captured in the blueprints and experience maps.

Service testing methods include **service staging**, **service walkthrough**, and **service role playing**. These techniques test the human, product, and spatial aspects of a service experience. Role-playing and staging help most with product and space to test journeys with mock-up or stand-in artifacts of the product, environment, and space layout. Users and customers walk through the scenarios and journeys, and you learn from their experiences and feedback. This learning is then used to iterate the designs further within project constraints.

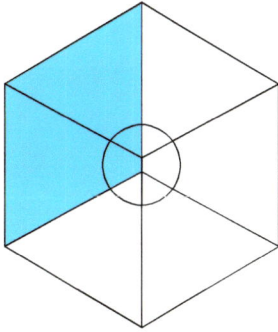

Delivery Phase

EXPERIENCE SPECIFICATION

The final phase in service design translates the design into actual delivery of the service experience. Once all journeys are designed to make up the experience lifecycle, you can specify the experience in detail so that hardware, software, events, and spaces can be built. The **service specification** focuses on what the experience for the customer and end user will be.

The specifications for hardware are mock-ups, drawings, and other documentation that specify the design, materials, and hardware components. For software, mobile, and web, the specifications are annotated wireframes, or screen schematics, that show clearly how the flow of content and functions work from a user's perspective, often combined with a set of HTML-coded visual pages.

For spaces, 3D renderings of the space are the usual specification. These do not replace building architectural drawings, but they concentrate on the experience of the user of the spaces and rooms inside a building. For hardware, software, and spaces, the design is captured as **service patterns** that reflect the experience framework of the service. These patterns capture reusable components of the service experience such as paths, hardware products, and how the users search, select, and navigate—both in software and spatially—

building signage design patterns. Depending on the collaborative nature of the delivery team, there may be more or less detailed specifications needed to support this phase.

All the above will benefit greatly from a **service experience guide** to more formally capture the service experience, so the experience can be replicated in different business contexts and applications. The guide keeps the design intent alive and ensures that the quality that you've reached in this particular service design can be replicated and built upon in future service experiences.

DELIVERY SUPPORT

During hardware development, software coding, and building engineering, ongoing help should be provided to maintain the intent of the experience. This is done with detailed **design support**, where the designers provide additional elements or replace elements where needed. This support decreases

more and more as you get closer to the release date of the service experience.

Throughout this step, conduct regular **QA and reviews** and from a service experience perspective. Monitor the quality of the experience, and provide input and recommendations to the solutions that are being built by the delivery team.

Finally, there should be an opportunity to conduct service **experience testing** at least once during the delivery phase. Through a combination of product experience testing (similar to user experience testing) and service walk-through testing of the space (plus products) with end users, you can catch service flow issues and address design concerns before service launch.

PART THREE

Experience Lifecycle Planning

Chapter 10

DESIGNING FOR THE END-TO-END EXPERIENCE LIFECYCLE

All brand, product, content, and service experiences shape your experience over time. This is the end-to-end experience lifecycle that begins with initial awareness and continues until ultimate disposal or cancellation. It's the sequence that the product/service goes through from first recognition to where it's replaced by a newer version, upgraded, expanded, discarded, or canceled altogether.

Connected Experiences

When you view the experience lifecycle from the audience's point of view, you create an overarching design framework that allows each experience to logically fit the appropriate moment in the lifecycle. You've created a holistic experience for your product or service.

With this lifecycle approach, the goal is to plan and design the experience in a coherent manner so the customer turned user will see and feel the experiences as being truly connected. When each lifecycle phase's experience is remarkable, you will grow customer loyalty, deliver your brand promise, and create deep advocacy for your product or service.

With an experience lifecycle, you map the experience from "cradle to grave" and take the connected experiences beyond the sales funnel, to optimize every "knot" on the red thread.

The Lifecycle Audiences

To design for the lifecycle, you need to understand your audience as they move through the lifecycle. As discussed earlier in this book, members of your audience change roles over time. The major roles are customer/citizen, user, and client. Although they may physically be the same person, they are quite different in terms of motivation and goals at various points in time.

Simply put, *customers* are people who buy; and their experience is formed through outreach, marketing, and facilitating the ultimate purchase decision. Their main goal is to understand the value and benefits of the offering and decide whether to engage or not. The customer traditionally gets much attention during experience design because

organizations are highly focused on getting the sale or onboarding the customer.

This is similar for public service situations where the customer role is fulfilled by the citizens. Although citizens aren't usually buying a product, they still need to become aware and go through a kind of onboarding process.

This early focus on the onboarding/purchase phase is critical and needs the appropriate design attention, but it shouldn't stop there. This phase is often intense, but it's relatively short compared to the overall duration of an experience lifecycle. The next phase begins once the customer owns the product, or starts to engage in the service. At this point, they become users.

Users are people who interact. Instead of identifying value, a user is concerned with completing a task—getting things done. For example, after you purchase your cell phone, you need to turn it on. Then you have to set it up, copy the backup from the old phone, set up the e-mail, and download updated apps. These activities have nothing to do with buying the product, getting value, or understanding the benefits. Users are no longer customers, and their journey is all about figuring things out.

Research shows that we're happiest right after we buy something, but soon our happiness is likely to decline. Organizationally speaking, this is because less effort is put in after the sale and onboarding, in order to keep the experience quality high. However, the customer's journey and the user's journey are different, so the experience design cannot start and end with the sale process. Both experiences contribute to the overall perception and experience with your brand and organization, so they should be designed independently and reflect the differences.

CUSTOMER

USER

CLIENT

It's all about extending the 'wow.' The 'wow' factor after the sale is what repeat purchases are based on. It's the reason for loyalty, long-term patronage, and peer recommendations. When every step in the lifecycle is addressed appropriately with enough budget and people, your users become loyal *clients*.

Loyalty signifies a long-standing beneficial relationship. This relationship comes with certain expectations that have formed over time as customers interact with the organization and their products and services. It's the highest goal for most organizations because keeping clients is more efficient than continuously finding new ones. In addition, loyal fans can be vocal fans and have a higher likelihood of recommending your offering to others. They may also have a greater reluctance to switch organizations, and they are more likely to buy your next remarkable product or service. All of these behaviors are the goal of good experience design.

The audience types described here play their part in the external/front-stage aspect of an experience lifecycle. In order for these experiences in the lifecycle to be successful, however, they must be enabled by internal/backstage organizational structures.

Simply put, good UX
is all about extending
the 'wow'.

The Experience Lifecycle

Understanding and capturing or mapping the experience lifecycle means following the red thread from learning about the product or service through all of the connected experience points, which are the knots on the thread. Each product or service will have a unique lifecycle that needs to be captured and used as the design framework for the detailed (product, content, brand, service) experiences that will make up the lifecycle.

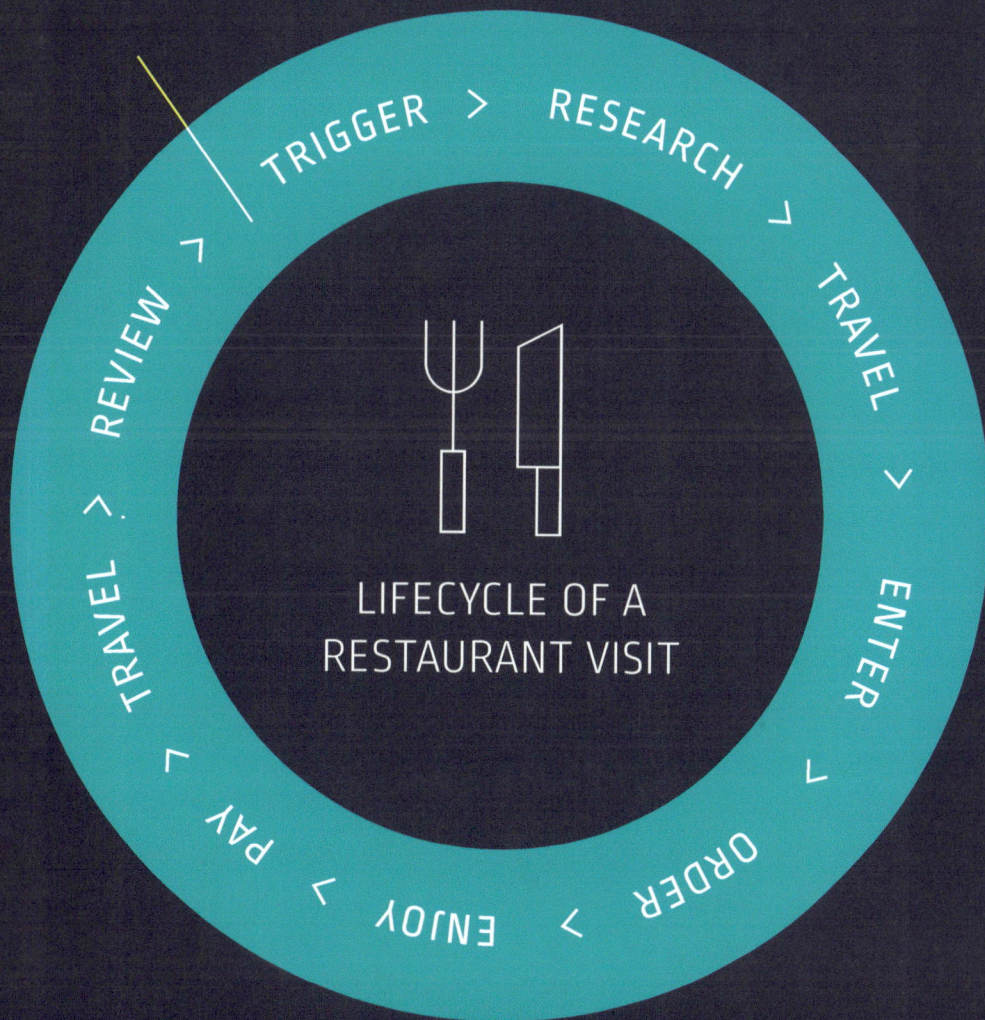

LIFECYCLE OF A
RESTAURANT VISIT

TRIGGER > RESEARCH > TRAVEL > ENTER > ORDER > ENJOY > PAY > TRAVEL > REVIEW >

End-to-end lifecycle example: Mobile phone

» **Become aware:** This is the first encounter with the product offering, usually through some form of marketing, advertising, seeing it in action in a store as you walk by, or a post by a loyal client on one of your social media feeds.

» **Research:** The customer acts on their interest to explore the value, benefits, and features of the product. At the same time, they become a user that explores. For example, they may search websites and storefronts for more information. They investigate other products to find comparable offerings, and also act as a user to find reviews and competitor information.

» **Purchase:** This is the point where the customer decides to buy and carries out the purchase transaction.

» **Unbox:** The customer now becomes a user at the first interaction with the physical packaging and by unpacking or taking the physical product out of the box.

» **Set up:** The user puts together the product components, sets up software, reads the manual if needed, or completes anything else necessary for setup.

» **Use:** This is when most of the product features are explored as the user becomes an expert in using the product. This period is measured differently, depending on the product or service. For example, it may only take minutes if you just unpacked a french fry carton, months if you are using one toothpaste tube, and years (hopefully) for mobile phones and furniture.

» **Maintain:** This phase occurs as the user keeps the product up and running. They may need to clean the product on a regular basis, troubleshoot, fix issues, or go through one or more support calls with the organization.

In both the use and maintain phases, the customer turns into a loyal client and an advocate for the product as they share their experiences and the reasons they love the product.

» **Upgrade:** Some products will go through this phase when accessories are added or capabilities are expanded.

» **Recycle or dispose:** The end of life for the product is when it's recycled for parts or disposed of responsibly. Assuming you would like to have a similar product, this is the point when the lifecycle starts again with the next generation of product offerings.

End-to-end lifecycle example: Driver's license

» **Become aware:** There is an initial encounter with the service offering in some form of marketing or advertising or through a post on one of your social media feeds.

» **Explore:** The customer/citizen acts on their interest to explore the value and benefits of the service. They become, at the same time, a user that explores. For example, they may visit websites, read leaflets, or call for more information.

» **Know:** The customer/citizen determines to move forward with the service. This differs from the for-profit compare phase that occurs at this point because public service organizations have little competition. It is just a matter of knowing the service is for you.

» **Apply:** This is the onboarding experience point where the customer/citizen engages and signs up for the service. It may or may not involve a monetary transaction.

» **Benefit:** The customer/citizen now becomes a user that benefits from the service in an ongoing way, such as being permitted to drive a car.

» **Renew:** In most cases, the service comes with an expiration date and will have to be renewed. For example, the user will renew their driver's license, reapply for a work permit, or demonstrate enough learning hours to stay within a professional association.

» **Replace:** Occasionally things don't go as planned. Something may happen that creates the need to redo or reorder in order to continue benefiting from the service as before. For example, a driver's license gets lost and needs to be replaced, or a password is forgotten that's

needed to update credit card information or keep paying for a subscription.

» **Cancel:** There is a point where the service isn't needed anymore and cancellation is required. For example, you may move to another city or country and have to cancel many services in short order (and start up the same kind of services in a different place).

More Lifecycle Examples

Each product and service will have it's own unique phases depending on the audience, service—your lifecycle is unique to your product and offering. The key is to conduct research to ensure understanding of what that lifecycle is.

MOBILE PHONE

AWARE > RESEARCH > PURCHASE > UNBOX > SET UP > USE > MAINTAIN > UPGRADE > RECYCLE

DRIVER'S LICENSE

AWARE > EXPLORE > KNOW > APPLY > BENEFIT > RENEW > REPLACE > CANCEL

INTERNET

AWARE > EXPLORE > COMPARE > SIGN UP > ENJOY > UPGRADE > MOVE

The Role of Experience Maps & Blueprints

Experience maps and experience blueprints are both part of a service experience design activity, and both have experience lifecycle phases. In fact, these lifecycle phases tie the two together and provide the anchor of the experience framework for each product and service created and supported by the organization.

The experience map focuses on the customer and user experience from the outside in. The map provides a terrific way to capture the experience journeys your customers and users have with the organization, without knowing exactly how things work within the organization. In many cases, teams are concerned with those experiences and want to design from that angle first.

The experience blueprint provides a more complete picture of how the organization's structure (people, process, technology, business) enables and supports the middle experiences (brand, product, content, service) that become the awesome end-to-end experiences in the lifecycle of those products and services. If experience lifecycles capture end-to-end, the experience blueprints capture how the organization delivers product and service value to external customers and internal employees from top to bottom.

The goal is to gain
understanding from
both the outside in
and the inside out.

Return on Experience

The business benefit of lifecycle thinking is apparent. By understanding and applying the end-to-end experience lifecycle to each experience point, you won't overlook any aspect of each customer or user experience. This is true whether a total experience lifecycle spans ten minutes (e.g., a french fry carton), a few years (e.g., software), or decades (e.g., a train to work or a government service). Most importantly, the end-to-end lifecycle of an experience ensures that both the organization (internal) view and the audience (external) view are represented in evaluating the *return on experience (ROX)*.

To evaluate the ROX, focus on what you want people to walk away with. How good is the overall experience? The ROX is not only a function of monetary investment or pure business goals. Instead, ask how the experience is working for your target audience. Are you retaining clients because of the experience? Are sales and loyalty numbers improving? The ROX is a lens through which to view and have meaningful conversations around product and service lifecycles, as well as to measure how successful your experience design could or should be. It may be measured by happy customers, retention, or revenue in for-profit organizations, or by engagement and recommendations in nonprofit groups.

Experiences Create Business Impact

When you approach experience design using the end-to-end lifecycle approach, you inevitably move into a human-centric design process. Creating an experience with this approach takes the risk out of investments by making sure that all of the design elements in the mix are known and well researched.

In order to create a positive experience, identify each element of the experience journey to uncover the characteristics and the relative importance of each one. In addition, both divergent and convergent thinking have a place in this process. You start very broadly, using exploratory techniques; then you converge into a solution phase. It's not a funnel that gets smaller and smaller the way you might want it to, however. You will be swimming in and out trying to identify what you're dealing with and then finding ways to improve it. The process feels uncomfortable at first, but the nature of experience design is dynamic. The more you practice it, the more

> Each knot in the red thread requires strategy, research, design, and testing in order to understand and create the end-to-end experience.

you will see the benefits. You become more at ease as you investigate and implement the lifecycle design of your product or service.

Building Loyalty Based on the Experience

An added benefit of creating a positive experience for your customer is that it builds loyalty. Loyalty is twofold in this context. First, it's an expression of connection and trust in the value that the customer always gets from your organization. Second, loyalty translates to action by your customer and causes them to behave differently.

Well-meaning companies may want to build trust, but they focus on the end goal of trust without articulating a path to get there. Unfortunately, loyalty is not created just by impact statements. You must actually plan how the trust will be built through the experiences you offer your customers and users. Whether trust is built by good service, good design, good staff, good value, or any

combination of the above, the good has to come first. Loyalty follows good experiences.

Building loyalty is an issue of experience, not communication. If you want to have loyal fans who are promoters of your business, you have to give them a reason to like you. The reason is not only a function of communication or branding; it's created by making your products and experience better. You are designing the experience throughout the lifecycle, from beginning to end, in such a balanced and in-depth way that people want to stay. Your customers will want to keep buying from you, engaging with you, and remaining a part of your ecosystem.

Loyalty is equally about connection and action.

PART FOUR

Implementation: Applying Experience Thinking

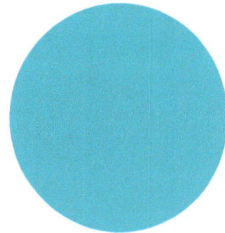

Chapter 11

ENGAGEMENT STRATEGIES FOR EXPERIENCE THINKING

It should be clear by this point in the book that Experience Thinking is a worthy aspiration for every organization. If practiced, the concept can feed your corporate culture and change the way you operate for the better.

Your Core Purpose

The starting point for the implementation of Experience Thinking in your organization is to stop for a moment and think about the core purpose of your business. What is it? How do you define yourself as an organization, and what do you offer? Smart companies realize that even if they have an interesting idea or an innovative offering, a core aspect of their business is the experience they deliver to their audience.

Engage Your Team & Organization

Once you embrace experience understanding and creation as a core capability, there are several ways to form your in-house team. The three most common models are centralized teams, decentralized teams, and matrix teams.

CENTRALIZED TEAMS

Having a centralized strategy simply means that you bring your team in-house and place them both physically and organizationally together. The team includes product/ service strategy consultants, customer/user researchers, and experience designers together with project and line management. The team may be as small as a half-dozen people, or as large as corporate groups in the hundreds.

The centralized approach allows you to start your own design and research department. You will bring diverse talents together in their own department to act as internal consultants to the larger organization. Although this is a workable strategy at first, different departments usually quickly overuse the designers as their own personal support. As soon as lines of business or departments understand and experience the value this team provides, there is often a risk of resource shortage.

The benefit of a centralized team is one of having peers that work beside you and a manager that understands your value and work. There is a real team, as all experience-related people work together. This is good for professional development and career progression.

As with any success, there is also a downside. The centralized department can be pulled into different business silos and end up too busy to be effective and responsive to the whole. Most of the time, a centralized team outsources the overflow work to external consultants, researchers, and designers. This creates the effect of the in-house team increasingly acting as business liaisons, account managers, or even project managers, but without the educational background or personal interest in acting in those roles.

This is the reason that many organizations then revert to the decentralized model.

DECENTRALIZED TEAMS

The decentralized model allocates designers and researchers to individual departments or lines of business. These smaller teams are embedded with the tech, content, and business people of that department; and both line management and project management are handled within the department. It often creates a tight team that can "do it all," as both design and tech are working together in the same place.

The risk is one of being managed by someone who doesn't have an experience design or research-related background, making it harder for a designer or researcher to learn and progress in the field. There is also a sense of being pegged as the expert in a specific product or service experience, limiting where the designer or researcher could work in the future. Being in a specific group also limits the ability to share the best practices in design and research with the rest of the organization.

Keeping your designers in different silos ignores opportunities to effectively connect each part of the overall customer journey or even the holistic experience lifecycle. To avoid this issue, enable communication tools and processes between silos, so your designers and researchers can effectively share and communicate with each other. The alternative is moving to a matrix approach.

MATRIX TEAMS

The matrix approach includes aspects of both the centralized and decentralized models.

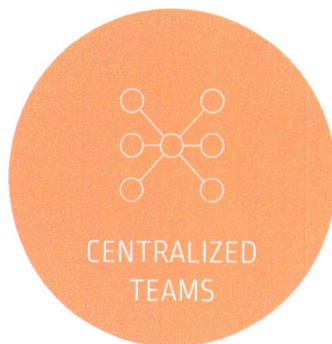

CENTRALIZED TEAMS

DECENTRALIZED TEAMS

MATRIX TEAMS

Designers and researchers are brought in-house in their own department, and then they are farmed out to specific departments, either on a project basis or as a temporary placement. They eventually return to the central team.

The central department is the keeper of the overall design and research approach, but stays nimble enough to manage and rotate resources on a project basis, in different silos. This approach is the best for maintaining the big-picture view of the overall experience design process while allowing the team to become enough of a domain expert to benefit different departments. In other words, you are maintaining a best-in-class centralized design and research process that is applied in different product domains and service departments.

In the end, each organization must balance their need for speed of delivery and quality of delivery. It's a trade-off between decentralized nimbleness and centralized best-in-class. What organizational structure fits best with

the shortest path to awesome experiences? Often, it's a matrix structure in some form.

Getting Started

The first project is the hardest, especially if you're starting from scratch and don't have an experience design and research team in place. Regardless of the model you ultimately find is the best fit for your organization, you should be applauded for taking these first steps.

It can feel overwhelming at first, so start small. Experiment by applying Experience Thinking to a known product or service with limited scope within your organization. Try using it as a lens for examining your existing product and service experiences and your approach to how you design the experience.

Take a good look within your organization before you start your first project. Investigate your organization, and assess its readiness to take on an Experience Thinking strategy. Does your current team have the skills to design and research experiences? Moreover, do they have the process knowledge to design and develop a customer or user experience? Knowing where your organization's current strengths and weaknesses lie helps you focus your people development and build your teams.

Ask yourself the following questions in the areas of design, technology, research, and management.

DESIGN

Does your team have a solid understanding of the latest product experience design and branding inside your organization?

Are you on top of the latest developments coming out of the organization?

If so, move forward to the next steps. If not, think about hiring your own designers or outsourcing your needs to an experience design company.

For any experience design team, you will need three distinct types of designers: a visual designer to create the emotional connection through visual product design; an interaction designer to flesh out navigation within the experience, including a focus on steps, tasks, scenarios, time, and so on; and a content and information architect to make sure the content is structured in a way that fulfills the user goals.

TECHNOLOGY

Do you have a solid understanding of the technology within your organization?

Do you know what is possible today with the technology you have in-house?

Do you know where things are going in the marketplace and what role new technology will have in your organization in the future?

If so, move forward. If not, hire a technology consultant to understand and foresee the technology landscape in the next one to three years.

RESEARCH

Do you have a solid understanding of behavioral psychology and customer behavior inside your organization?

Do you know and have evidence to back up how your audience uses your website, your product, or your service?

This is important not only at the value and benefit level, but also at the "doing" level.

Do you have a clear picture of a day in the life of a user, including what they do with your product or service, when they do it, and where it occurs?

If yes, move forward. If not, hire a researcher to gather this data, and give them the opportunity to turn it into deep insights that you can use in the design phase.

The best consultant in this area would be a research consultant with a background in human behavior sciences and a business affinity. Researchers should be able to handle usability testing sessions and come up with strategies to define the right product or service. These roles require interviewing, observation, and task analysis.

MANAGEMENT

Are you ready to manage a holistic experience design project?

If so, great! Move forward. If not, seek assistance for your first project. The project manager needs familiarity with the design process to be successful.

For many organizations, experience design is a new discipline. Don't be afraid to bring in more C-suite level and senior people that know the process and can take the lead in executing it. Define and capture your design process, and share it with the organization from the top down. Then bring in junior researchers, designers, and tech experts to backfill and grow your teams.

This change management process will take a couple of years to see real change and progress at a company culture level. Once it happens, though, it's hard (if not impossible) to go back. The aha moments going through the experience design process will leave lasting impressions on the people that participate. It's one of those "why didn't I see this before" or "why wouldn't you do it this way" types of learning experiences.

Chapter 12

EMBRACING EXPERIENCE THINKING

Experience encompasses everything—time, space, flow, immersion, participation, feelings, transformation. Organizations that start with the experience and let it be their driving force will reap the benefits, and those that don't will simply be left behind. Since many of your competitors understand the value in creating the experience, it has become more than just a good idea.

AUDIENCE
Customers, Citizens, Users, Employees

EXPERIENCE LIFECYCLE

TECHNOLOGY

PROCESS

BUSINESS

PEOPLE
Partners, Suppliers, Internal Team

It's easy to give lip service to the idea that experience matters. You may have said, "We have to streamline the experience, we have to make it better, and we have to make it seamless." These are noble thoughts, but you have to take steps organizationally and specifically in the areas of research and design to execute your grand plan.

Make experience design a part of your core business, and give it the same attention you give other core departments. When Experience Thinking becomes a fundamental organizational principle and belief, you will see the value in treating design the same way as you treat engineering, technology, or content.

All organizations start with a business model and enabling technologies. When these can be transformed into something experiential in the realms of brand, engagement, content, product, and service, your users will become loyal clientele. The customer's journey will feel connected and complete, by design.

Experience design isn't new, and it's not a magic formula. Every successful project involves design, technology, and people research. It's really business as usual when you think about it. But if you can bring the strengths of Experience Thinking into your organization at every point in the project lifecycle, you will produce better and more predictable experiences sooner. Seems like a smart choice!

When you understand the principle of experience design and prioritize the Experience Thinking approach, the benefits are clear: reduced time to market, more successful products, and loyal customers willing to sing your praises. I hope you get started soon on this journey to awesome.

It's the shortest path to remarkable experiences.

www.ingramcontent.com/pod-product-compliance
Lightning Source LLC
Chambersburg PA
CBHW042132040426

42336CB00038B/42